The Plutarch Project

Volume Two

The Plutarch Project
Volume Two

Pyrrhus, Nicias, and Crassus

by

Anne E. White

ISBN-13 978-0-9947977-6-6

CONTENTS

Introduction

These notes, and the accompanying text, are based on Thomas North's 1579 translation of Plutarch's *Lives of the Noble Greeks and Romans*, with some substitutions from John Dryden's 1683 translation [in brackets]. I have updated spelling, and occasionally punctuation. There are also a number of omissions, either for length or for suitability, which are *not* always noted. I have tried to be respectful to Plutarch's text, but have amplified and clarified where it seemed helpful for students and parents/teachers.

The format of the study notes is fairly simple. Each *Life* is divided into twelve lessons (as the AmblesideOnline[1] terms are divided into twelve weeks). I have included vocabulary words and narration/study questions, but there is no requirement that you use them in a traditional classroom style. In fact, it's probably better if you don't. The vocabulary words are there only to save time on having to look things up, or to explain puzzles like the word "let," which can mean either "allow" or "prevent." Charlotte Mason mentions teaching a few necessary words before beginning a story, such as unfamiliar types of buildings or weapons (with pictures if necessary). The *Life of Pyrrhus* includes a bonus **Word Study** feature.

Those following Charlotte Mason's educational methods will want to include oral or written narration (telling back in the student's own words), and oral narration can take place more than once during a lesson. (I used to stop during a reading and ask whichever daughter was listening, "What just happened there?" With Plutarch's long sentences, even I wasn't always sure.) Sometimes I have suggested a "creative narration," such as an interview or a writing assignment.

Using the Study Guide

Some of the lessons are divided into two or three sections. These can be read all at once, or used throughout the week.

I encourage you to make the lessons your own. Use the discussion questions that are the most meaningful to you, and skip the rest. It's better if the students ask the questions, at least some of the time. And remember that Charlotte Mason was satisfied with "Proper names are written on the blackboard, and then the children narrate what they have listened to."

Finally, you may notice that some of the questions come from a specifically Christian worldview. I do not apologize for that, but I do think it's fair to mention it. Those with other beliefs may find similar references within their own faith traditions.

Notes

1. AmblesideOnline is a free, online Charlotte Mason homeschooling curriculum, found at www.amblesideonline.org.

Why Plutarch?

(reprinted from *Minds More Awake*)

The decision to include Plutarch's *Lives*—or not—or in what translation—becomes a kind of touchpoint for how we view (or do) a Charlotte Mason education. Shakespeare is easy; everyone knows Shakespeare, recognizes Shakespeare. Nobody argues with teaching Shakespeare. But Plutarch belongs much more unmistakably to Charlotte Mason. If homeschooling was the world and Charlotte Mason was Canada, Plutarch would be maple syrup. We need to ask, and it's a fair question, if this was just one of those quaint turn-of-the-century ideas, like making Smyrna rugs for handicrafts; if Plutarch's *Lives* is essential in itself, or if what it offers could much more easily be acquired through newer books. Why did Charlotte Mason include this particular piece of antiquity?

Here are some of the reasons that Mason gave herself, or that were noted by her colleagues:

1) In the preface to *Ourselves*, she wrote that the novels of Sir Walter Scott and Plutarch's *Lives* were "sources that fall within everybody's reading." This is obviously not the case now, but at one time, Plutarch was considered common currency. Shakespeare read Plutarch. Abraham Lincoln read Plutarch. Frankenstein's monster read Plutarch. Ralph Waldo Emerson begins his essay on Plutarch with the words, "It is remarkable that of an author so familiar as Plutarch, not only to scholars, but to all reading men..." Plutarch is not studied in most contemporary schools, at least below university level, but he was less obscure in previous eras than we may realize.

2) Similarly, the introduction of Plutarch at what seems a younger-than-necessary age was explained in *Parents and Children*[1] as part of a plan that brings a child to the world's library door, and offers him the key to its contents. (It is worth noting that Mason mentions only two books in that passage: *Tanglewood Tales* for young children, and then Plutarch's *Lives*.) We don't just hand the child these books; we read them to him, but without too much

explanation, a gift from one book-loving friend to another. We read, he narrates, we discuss, but we do not limit what he learns to our own ideas about it. My own prepared notes might seem to be at cross-purposes with Mason's "pick it up and read" attitude, but I justify them with the hope that they will encourage those of us (including myself) who did not grow up with Plutarch...

3) As well as an early beginning to literature and the habit of reading in general, Plutarch offers "the best preparation for the study of Grecian or of Roman history."[2] Note that Mason said preparation for history, not history itself. It is a familiarizing, a paving of the way. After reading several *Lives*, we begin to recognize not only the characters, but also common events such as the annual election of Roman consuls...

4) The book *In Memoriam* says that Charlotte Mason lived during an age that was fascinated by history, but that her "standards of judgement were ethical" and that "greatness in goodness was her ideal..."[3] Miss Ambler, the author of a *Parents' Review* article on teaching Plutarch, agreed:

> We need, however, to have more than a goal
> in view; we need to know the way to reach
> it. We know what is necessary for a good
> citizen, and we wish to send the children out
> equipped for service with high ideals and the
> courage to live up to them.[4]

Notes

1. Charlotte Mason, *Parents and Children*, pp.231-232.

2. Charlotte Mason, *Home Education*, p.286.

3. *In Memoriam*, Parents' National Educational Union, 1923. http://www.amblesideonline.org/CM/InMemoriam.html

4. Miss M. Ambler, "'Plutarch's Lives' as Affording Some Education as a Citizen," *The Parents' Review*, 12 (1901): 521-527, AmblesideOnline

Pyrrhus
(319/318–272 B.C.)

"Whilst he lived, he was ever esteemed the chiefest
of all the kings and princes in his time, as well for
his experience and sufficiency in wars, as also for
the valiantness and hardiness of his person."

"Fabricius softly giving back, nothing afraid,
laughed and said to Pyrrhus, smiling: Neither did
your gold (oh king) yesterday move me, nor your
elephant today fear me."

The World of Pyrrhus

One of the authors read in the AmblesideOnline Curriculum is
Genevieve Foster. Her books such as *George Washington's World* and
Augustus Caesar's World describe not only a main character, but others
of the same time whose lives intertwined. The *Life of Pyrrhus* is also
such a broad-ranging story.

The background begins four or five years before the birth of
Pyrrhus, with the death of Alexander the Great in 323 B.C. and the
breakup of his empire. The world in which Pyrrhus grew up was
caught between four "power blocks": Ptolemaic Egypt,
Mesopotamia/Central Asia (the Seleucid Empire), Anatolia, and

Macedon. His own people (those of the Greek state of **Epirus**) had allied themselves with **Macedon**. (If you are interested in researching this further, look up the "Wars of the Diadochi.")

When Pyrrhus was born, his father **Æacides (Alcetus II)** was king of Epirus, but he was dethroned soon after, leaving small Pyrrhus as something like Charlotte M. Yonge's *Little Duke*, under the protection of friends.

Pyrrhus came into his adult life around the year 300 B.C. Although he had been restored as king briefly, he was deposed again by his father's enemy Cassander. He was then sent to Egypt, after a battle between several kings. However, that wasn't all bad, because Pyrrhus began a friendly relationship with King Ptolemy, Queen Berenice, and their daughter Antigone/Antigona, who became his first wife. Ptolemy also helped to restore Pyrrhus once again to the throne of Epirus, when Cassander died a short time later.

A rival (and relative), Neoptolemus II, complicated the return of Pyrrhus, but the conflict was temporarily settled by making the two men co-rulers. As one might expect, though, such a solution would not last.

The Rise of Rome

Pyrrhus fought with surprising success against the Roman legions. However, Rome was quickly gaining power across the Mediterranean, and it was only a matter of time before Rome would rule all the Greek city-states.

Was Pyrrhus a good ruler?

Pyrrhus was skillful and courageous, but not always wise. He is, unfortunately, remembered by the term "pyrrhic victory," meaning one in which heavy losses are sustained. Pyrrhus himself said, after that battle, "If we win another of the price, we are utterly undone."

How do you spell Pyrrhus?

North's translation spells it "Pyrrus," but other English translations (including Dryden) use the spelling "Pyrrhus." I have used the more common spelling.

What was Epirus? Who were the Epirotes?

Epirus was (and is) a region of southeastern Europe, now shared between modern-day Greece and Turkey. The **Epirotes** had a different lifestyle and language from other Greeks; they were a sort of border culture, out in the Greek "boonies." However, they did possess a famous shrine and oracle.

Who was Ptolemy?

Ptolemy I Soter ("Ptolemy the Saviour") was a Macedonian general and close friend of Alexander the Great, and became ruler of Egypt after Alexander's death. He lived from about 367-283 B.C., so he was quite a bit older than Pyrrhus. Pyrrhus named his oldest son after Ptolemy.

Trivia question: What famous mathematician was active in Ptolemy's court at Alexandria? The answer will appear at the end of **Lesson One.**

Who was Cassander?

He lived from about 350-297 B.C., and was king of Macedon for several years. He had been a student of Aristotle, along with Alexander the Great. His father, Antipater, had also been a close friend of Alexander. The struggle between Cassander's widow (Thessalonica, a half-sister of Alexander) and their sons is mentioned later in the story.

The sons of Cassander

Cassander's sons were Antipater II and Alexander V of Macedon. Antipater was killed by Lysimachus (during events not mentioned here), and Alexander was murdered by Demetrius in 294 B.C.

Who was Lysimachus?

Lysimachus (accent on the "sim") was king of Thrace. He died in battle in 281 B.C., just before Pyrrhus invaded southern Italy.

Who was Demetrius?

Demetrius I Poliorcetes is the subject of Plutarch's *Life of Demetrius*. He lived from 337-283 B.C., making him about twenty years older than Pyrrhus; he was the son of Antigonus I Monopthalmus, one of Alexander's generals. In 294 B.C., he declared himself king of Macedon.

Who was Antigonus?

Antigonus II Gonatus was the son of Demetrius I, but his succession as king was interrupted by the ongoing wars over Macedon.

Lesson One

Introduction

This lesson begins with mythology, as far back as Deucalion (the Greek version of Noah). The ancestors named in Part One will not have meaning for most students, so it might be better to introduce the lesson with information about Epirus. The family of Pyrrhus had deep roots in that part of Greece, but the country had become "barbarous," without recorded history.

Vocabulary

> **civility, civil:** see the **Word Study** section
>
> **posterity:** generations
>
> **drave:** drove
>
> **lusty:** healthy and strong
>
> **a certain city of Macedon, called Megares:** the better-known city of Megara is in the south of Greece; this was another with the same name
>
> **made stay of:** held back

weening: supposing

gauged the ford: judged how safe it would be to cross the river

the tongue of a buckle: the sharp part that goes through the holes

residue: remainder

the altar of the familiar gods: the family altar

by god's providence: it is not clear which god or gods he is referring to

thereunto: (to) that

that great battle...: the Battle of Ipsus

People

the Molossians: a founding tribe of Epirus

Æacides: Alcetus II, the father of Pyrrhus and king of Epirus

Achilles: significant in Part Two because the name Achilles was revered in Epirus

Glaucias, king of Illyria: sometimes spelled Glaukias. He ruled from 335-c. 302 B.C.

Neoptolemus: Neoptolemus II, cousin of Pyrrhus and nephew of Alexander the Great; born 331 B.C.

Historic Occasions

301 B.C.: the Battle of Ipsus

Reading

Part One (optional)

It is written, that since [the flood], the first king of the Thesprotians, and of **the Molossians**, was Phaëton, one of those who came with Pelasgus, into the realm of Epirus. But some say otherwise, that Deucalion, and his wife Pyrrha remained there, after they had built

9

and founded the temple of Dodone, in the country of **the Molossians**. But howsoever it was, a great while after that, Neoptolemus the son of Achilles [*yes, that Achilles*], bringing thither a great number of people with him, conquered the country, and after him left a succession of kings, which were called after his name, the Pyrrides: because that from his infancy he was surnamed Pyrrhus, as much to say as "red": and one of his sons whom he had by Lanassa, the daughter of Cleodes, the son of Hillus, was also named by him Pyrrhus [*not our Pyrrhus, this is long before*]. And this is the cause why Achilles is honoured as a god in Epirus, being called in their language, *Aspetos*, that is to say, mighty, or very great.

Part Two

But from the first kings of that race until the time of Tharrytas [Dryden: *Tharrhypas*], there is no memory nor mention made of [their lives], nor of their power that reigned in the meantime, because they all became very barbarous, and utterly void of **civility**. Tharrytas was indeed the first that beautified the cities of his country with the Grecian tongue, brought in **civil** laws and customs, and made his name famous to the **posterity** that followed.

This Tharrytas left a son called Alcetas; of Alcetas came Arymbas [*or Arrybas*], of Arymbas and Troiade his wife, came **Æacides,** who married Phthia, the daughter of Menon Thessalian. This **Æacides** had two daughters by his wife Phthia, to say, Deidamia and Troiade, and one son called Pyrrhus.

In his time **the Molossians** rebelled, **drave** him out of his kingdom, and put the crown into the hands of the sons of Neoptolemus. Whereupon all the friends of **Æacides** that could be taken, were generally murdered, and slain outright. Androclides and Angelus in the meantime stole away Pyrrhus, being yet but a suckling babe (whom his enemies nevertheless eagerly sought for to have destroyed) and fled away with him as fast as possibly they might, with few servants, his nurses and necessary women only to look to the child, and give it suck: by reason whereof [*taking care of the baby*] their flight was much hindered, so as they could go no great journeys, but that they might easily be overtaken by them that followed. For which cause they put the child into the hands of Androclion, Hippias, and Neander, three **lusty** young men, whom they trusted with him, and commanded them to run for life to **a certain city of Macedon, called Megares** [*Dryden: Megara*]: and they themselves in the meantime, partly by entreaty, and partly by force, **made stay of** those that followed them till night.

So as with much ado having driven them back, they ran after them that carried the child Pyrrhus, whom they overtook at sunset. And now, **weening** they had been safe, and out of all danger: they found it clean contrary. For when they came to the river under the town walls of Megares, they saw it so rough and swift, that it made them afraid to behold it: and when they **gauged the ford**, they found it unpossible to wade through, it was so sore risen and troubled with the fall of the rain, besides that the darkness of the night made every thing seem fearful unto them.

So as they now that carried the child, thought it not good to venture the passage over [by] themselves alone, with the women that tended the child: but hearing certain countrymen on the other side, they prayed and besought them in the name of the gods, that they would help them to pass over the child, showing Pyrrhus unto them afar off. But the countrymen by reason of the roaring of the river understood them not. Thus they continued a long space, the one crying, the other listening, yet could they not understand one another, till at the last one of the company bethought himself to pull off a piece of the bark of an oak, and upon that he wrote with **the tongue of a buckle**, the hard fortune and necessity of the child. Which he tied to a stone to give it weight, and so threw it over to the other side of the river. Others say that he did prick the bark through with the point of a dart which he cast over.

The countrymen on the other side of the river, having read what was written, and understanding thereby the present danger the child was in, felled down trees in all the haste they could possibly, bound them together, and so [the men] passed over the river. And it fortuned that the first man of them that passed over, and took the child, was called **Achilles**: the **residue** of the countrymen passed over also, and took the other that came with the child, and conveyed them over as they came first to hand.

And thus having escaped their hands, by easy journeys they came at the length unto **Glaucias, king of Illyria**, whom they found in his house sitting by his wife: and [they] laid down the child in the midst of the floor before him. The king hereupon stayed a long time without uttering any one word, weighing with himself what was best to be done: because of the fear he had of Cassander, a mortal enemy of **Æacides**. In the meantime, the child Pyrrhus, creeping [on] all fours, took hold of the king's gown and crawled up by that, and so got up on his feet against the king's knees. At the first, the king laughed to see the child: but after it [he] pitied him again, because the child seemed like a humble suitor that came to seek sanctuary in his arms. Other[s] say that Pyrrhus came not to Glaucias, but unto **the altar of the familiar gods**, alongst the which he got up on his feet, and embraced it with both his hands. Which Glaucias imagining to be done **by god's providence**, presently delivered the child to his wife, gave her the charge of him, and willed her to see him brought up with his own.

Shortly after, his enemies sent to demand the child of him: and moreover, Cassander caused two hundred talents to be offered him, to deliver the child Pyrrhus into his hands. Howbeit Glaucias would never grant **thereunto**, but contrarily, when Pyrrhus was come to twelve years old, brought him into his country of Epirus with an army, and [e]stablished him [as] king of the realm again.

Part Three

Now, when he was seventeen years of age, the Molossians rebelled again against him, and **drave** out his friends, and servants, and destroyed all his goods, and yielded themselves unto his adversary **Neoptolemus**. King Pyrrhus having thus lost his kingdom, and seeing himself forsaken on all sides, went to Demetrius (Antigonus' son) that had married his sister Deidamia.

And in **that great battle which was stricken near to the city of Hipsus,** where all the kings fought together, Pyrrhus being then but a young man, and with Demetrius, put them all to flight that fought with him. And afterwards when peace was concluded betwixt Demetrius and Ptolemy, Pyrrhus was sent [as] a hostage for Demetrius into the realm of Egypt: where he made Ptolemy know (both in hunting, and in other exercises of his person) that he was very strong, hard, and able to endure any labour. Furthermore perceiving that Berenice amongst all King Ptolemy's wives, was best beloved and esteemed of her husband, both for her virtue and wisdom: he began to entertain and honour her above all the rest. For he was a man that could tell how to humble himself towards the great (by whom he might win benefit) and knew also how to creep into their credit: and in like manner was he a great scorner and despiser of such as were his inferiors. Moreover, for that he was found marvellous honourable and of fair condition, he was preferred before all other young princes, to be the husband of Antigona, the daughter of Queen Berenice, whom she had by Philip, before she was married unto Ptolemy.

Word Study

Civility, civil: These words come from the Latin root **civ,** meaning a citizen, a person who lives in a condition of social order and under an organized government. **Civil** can refer to anything that has to do with the organization of citizens; or it can also mean courteous and mannerly (as opposed to **barbaric,** boorish, churlish). What does it mean if a person is a **civilian?** What is a **civil** war?

Narration and Discussion

Why was King Glaucias interested in seeing Pyrrhus restored to his rightful throne?

How are Pyrrhus' experiences as a young man somewhat similar to those of Joseph or Moses (in the Old Testament)?

"For he was a man that could tell how to humble himself towards the great (by whom he might win benefit) and knew also how to creep into their credit: and in like manner was he a great scorner and despiser of such as were his inferiors." Did these characteristics predict success, trouble, or both?

(Answer to the trivia question: Euclid.)

Lesson Two

Introduction

Co-ruling sometimes works well, as in the consul system of Rome. And sometimes it does not. Pyrrhus returned to Epirus, but he did not get on very well with his cousin and fellow king Neoptolemus. In fact, he discovered that Neoptolemus was trying to kill him.

Vocabulary

From thenceforth growing through the alliance of that marriage, more and more into estimation...: Pyrrhus' marriage to Antigona made him more popular and powerful (see also **Word Study**)

hardly: severely

repair: go

Iupiter Martial: Dryden translates this "Mars"

interchangeably: This is not fully explained, but I think that, in the case of co-rulers, the friends of each king would swear loyalty and give gifts to the other one; which would explain why Gelon, a supporter of Neoptolemus, gave a pair of oxen to Pyrrhus. "Interchangeably" might also refer to the giving and receiving, e.g. why Myrtilus then asked Pyrrhus for the oxen (which might seem rude to us).

pretended: intended

saving: except for

made no countenance of anything: said little about it

dispatch: get rid of, kill

in the Prescque...: Dryden, "in the Peninsula of Epirus." The actual location of the city seems to be unknown.

for his charge sustained: for his services

added unto it by force of arms: new conquests

put good garrisons into the same...: he brought in his own soldiers

towards the defraying of his charges: as payment for the expense he
had incurred

fetch and device: trick

to be sworn upon the sacrifices...: to confirm the peace with an oath

People

Cassander, etc.: see notes at the beginning of the study

Historic Occasions

294 B.C.: "Alexander's Wars" ended with the murder of Alexander by
Demetrius (omitted here for length)

Reading

Part One

**From thenceforth growing through the alliance of that
marriage, more and more into estimation and favour by means
of his wife Antigona,** who shewed herself very virtuous and loving
towards him: he found means in the end, to get both men and money
to return again into the realm of Epirus, and to conquer it: so was he
then very well received of the people, and the better for the malice
they bare to Neoptolemus, because he [Neoptolemus] dealt both
hardly and cruelly with them. That notwithstanding, Pyrrhus, fearing
lest Neoptolemus would **repair** unto some of the other kings to seek
aid against him, thought good to make peace with him. Whereupon it
was agreed between them, that they should both together be kings of
Epirus.

But in process of time, some of their men secretly made strife
again between them, and set them at defiance one with another: and
the chiefest cause as it is said, that angered Pyrrhus most, grew upon
this. The kings of Epirus had an ancient custom of great antiquity,
after they had made solemn sacrifice unto **Iupiter Martial,** (in a
certain place in the province of Molosside, called Passaron) to take

their oath, and to be sworn to the Epirotes, that they would reign well and justly, according to the laws and ordinances of the country: and to receive the subjects' oaths **interchangeably** also, that they would defend and maintain them in their kingdom, according to the laws in like manner. This ceremony was done in the presence of both the kings, and they with their friends did both give and receive presents of each other.

At this meeting and solemnity, among other[s], one Gelon, a most faithful servant and assured friend unto Neoptolemus, who besides great shows of friendship and honour he did unto Pyrrhus, gave him two pairs of draught oxen, which one Myrtilus a cupbearer of Pyrrhus being present, and seeing, did crave of his master. But Pyrrhus denied to give them unto him, whereat Myrtilus was very angry. Gelon perceiving that Myrtilus was angry, prayed him to sup with him that night. [He] began to persuade him after supper to take part with Neoptolemus, and to poison Pyrrhus. Myrtilus made as though he was willing to give ear to this persuasion, and to be well pleased withal. But in the meantime, he went and told his master of it, by whose commandment he made Alexicrates, Pyrrhus' chief cupbearer, to talk with Gelon about this practise, as though he had also given his consent to it, and was willing to be partaker of the enterprise. This did Pyrrhus to have two witnesses, to prove the **pretended** poisoning of him.

Thus Gelon being finely deceived, and Neoptolemus also with him, both imagining they had cunningly spun the thread of their treason: Neoptolemus was so glad of it, that he could not keep it to himself, but told it to certain of his friends. And on a time going to be merry with his sister, he could not keep it in, but must be prattling of it to her, supposing nobody had heard him but herself, because there was no living creature near them, **saving** Phoenareta, Samon's wife, the king's chief herdman of all his beasts, and yet she was laid upon a little bed [near]by, and turned towards the wall: so that she seemed as though she had slept. But having heard all their talk, and nobody mistrusting her: the next morning she went to Antigona, King Pyrrhus' wife, and told her every word what she had heard Neoptolemus say to his sister.

Pyrrhus hearing this, **made no countenance of anything** at that time. But having made sacrifice unto the gods, he bade Neoptolemus to supper to his house, where he slew him, being well informed before of the good will the chiefest men of the realm did bear him, who wished him to **dispatch** Neoptolemus, and not to content himself with a piece of Epirus only, but to follow his natural inclination, being born to great things: and for this cause therefore, this suspicion [of Neoptolemus] falling out in the meanwhile, he prevented Neoptolemus, and slew him first.

And furthermore, remembering the pleasures he had received of Ptolemy and Berenice, he named his first son by his wife Antigona, Ptolemy, and having built a city **in the Prescque, an Isle of Epirus**, did name it Berenicida. When he had done that, imagining great matters in his head, but more in his hope, he first determined with himself how to win that which lay nearest unto him: and so took occasion by this means, first to set foot into the Empire of Macedon.

Part Two

The eldest son of Cassander [the king of Macedonia], called Antipater, put his own mother Thessalonica to death, and drave his brother Alexander out of his own country, who sent to Demetrius for help, and called in Pyrrhus also to his aid.

Demetrius, being troubled with other matters, could not so quickly go thither. And Pyrrhus being arrived there, demanded, **for his charge sustained,** the city of Nymphæa, with all the sea coasts of Macedon: and besides all that, certain lands also that were not belonging to the ancient crown and revenues of the kings of Macedon, but were **added unto it by force of arms**, as Ambracia, Acarnania, and Amphilochia. All these, the young King Alexander leaving unto him, he took possession thereof, and **put good garrisons into the same in his own name**: and conquering the rest of Macedon in the name of Alexander, put his brother Antipater to great distress.

In the meantime King Lysimachus lacked no good will to help Antipater with his force, but being busied in other matters, had not the mean[s] to do it. Howbeit knowing very well that Pyrrhus in acknowledging the great pleasures he had received of Ptolemy, would deny him nothing: he determined to write counterfeit letters to him in Ptolemy's name, and thereby instantly to pray and require him to leave off the wars begun against Antipater, and to take, **towards the defraying of his charges**, the sum of three hundred talents.

Pyrrhus opening the letters, knew straight that this was but a **fetch and device** of Lysimachus. For King Ptolemy's common manner of greeting of him, which he used at the beginning of his letters, was not in them observed: *To my son Pyrrhus, health.* But in those counterfeit was, *King Ptolemy, unto King Pyrrhus, health.* Whereupon he presently pronounced Lysimachus for a naughty man.

Part Three

Nevertheless, afterwards he made peace with Antipater, and they met together at a day appointed, **to be sworn upon the sacrifices unto the articles of peace.**

There were three beasts brought to be sacrificed, a goat, a bull, and a ram: of the which, the ram fell down dead of himself before he was touched, whereat all the standers-by fell a-laughing. But there was a soothsayer, one Theodotus, that persuaded Pyrrhus not to swear: saying, that this sign and token of the gods did threaten one of the three kings with sudden death. For which cause Pyrrhus concluded no peace.

Word Study

Estimation: Have you noticed the connection between our use of **estimation** (what you do when you're guesstimating size, time, or amount of something) and **esteem**? The words come from a Latin root meaning "to value, to appraise the worth of" and they also are closely connected with "to judge." The use of **estimation** to mean "making an approximate measurement" began in the 17th century.

Narration and Discussion

Why did Pyrrhus think it would be a better idea to rule alongside Neoptolemus than to overthrow him?

In a passage that was omitted, Dryden's translation speaks of "the innate disease of princes, ambition of greater empire." (Innate means natural, instinctive.) Why do you think he chose the word "disease?" Did Pyrrhus have this disease?

Lesson Three

Introduction

In a between-lessons section omitted for length, Pyrrhus and Demetrius each claimed part of Macedon. In preparing to battle over it, they carried out a "comedy of errors," as they each missed their way to the meeting point. Demetrius ended up in Epirus and settled for making some raids. Pyrrhus fought a Macedonian general, and, though wounded, he gave back twice as much, and took five thousand prisoners.

This lesson begins with ruminations on the character and "valiantness" of Pyrrhus. A temporary state of peace between the Epirotes and the Macedonians would not last long; and there were threats from other countries as well, particularly against Demetrius (which encouraged Pyrrhus to look for his own opportunities).

Vocabulary

counterfeit: copy (see also **Word Study**)

the books he wrote himself thereof: these books no longer exist

requite: pay back

for her dower: for her dowry, a wedding present to her husband

Isle of Corfu: a Greek island in the Ionian Sea (see **Corfu or Corcyra?**)

martial: military, warlike

such opportunity and occasion: the chance to invade Macedonia

tarry and fight with him for the altars, temples, and sepulchres of the Molossians: If Pyrrhus waited too long, Demetrius might bring the war into Epirus and cause destruction there..

garrison: military troops; protection

tracted time: delayed things

Berroea: a town in Macedonia (Dryden: Beroea)

his horse Nisea: a mistranslation by North; it should be a Nisean or Nisaean horse (a breed that is now extinct)

People

Autoleon, king of Paeonia: also spelled Audoleon

Agathocles: the ruler of Syracuse (a Greek colony in Sicily), and king of Sicily

Ptolemy, Lysimachus, etc.: see notes at the beginning

Historic Occasions

291 B.C.: Lanassa left her husband Pyrrhus for Demetrius

Corfu or Corcyra?

The island of Corfu is located off the coast of Epirus. Corfu is the more modern word; Dryden's translation uses "Corcyra."

Reading

Part One

This overthrow did not so much fill the hearts of the Macedonians with anger, for the loss they had received, nor with the hate conceived against Pyrrhus: as it won Pyrrhus great fame and honour, making his courage and valiantness to be wondered at of all such as were present at the battle that saw him fight, and how he laid about him. For they thought that they saw in his face the very life and agility of Alexander the Great, and the right shadow as it were, showing the force and fury of Alexander himself in that fight. And where other kings did but only **counterfeit** Alexander the Great in his purple garments, and in numbers of soldiers and guards about their persons, and in a certain fashion and bowing of their necks a little, and in uttering his speech with an high voice: Pyrrhus only was like unto him, and followed him in his martial deeds and valiant acts.

Furthermore, for his experience and skill in warlike discipline, **the books he wrote himself thereof**, do amply prove and make manifest.

Furthermore, they report, that King Antigonus being asked whom he thought to be the greatest captain: made answer, "Pyrrhus, so far forth as he might live to be old," speaking only of the captains of his time. But Hannibal generally said, Pyrrhus was the greatest captain of experience and skill in wars of all other, Scipio the second, and himself the third: as we have written in the *Life of Scipio*.

So it seemeth that Pyrrhus gave his whole life and study to the discipline of wars, as that which indeed was princely and meet for a king, making no reckoning of all other knowledge. And furthermore touching this matter, they report that he being at a feast one day, a question was asked him, whom he thought to be the best player of the flute, Python or Cephesias: whereunto he answered, that Polyperchon in his opinion was the best captain, as if he would have said, that was the only thing a prince should seek for, and which he ought chiefly to learn and know.

He was very gentle and familiar with his friends, easy to forgive when any had offended him, and marvellous desirous to **requite** and acknowledge any courtesy or pleasure by him received.

After the death of Antigona, he married many wives to increase his power withal, and to get more friends. For he married the daughter of Autoleon, king of Paeonia, and Bircenna the daughter of Bardillis, king of Illyria, and Lanassa, the daughter of Agathocles, tyrant of Syracuse, that brought him **for her dower** the **Isle of Corfu**, which her father had taken. By Antigona his first wife, he [Pyrrhus] had a son called Ptolemy: By Lanassa, another called Alexander: and by Bircenna, another (the youngest of all) called Helenus: all which though they were **martial** men by race and natural inclination, yet were they brought up by him in wars, and therein trained as it were even from their cradle.

They write, that one of his sons, being but a boy, asked him one day to which of them he would leave his kingdom: Pyrrhus answered the boy, "To him that hath the sharpest sword." That was much like the tragical curse wherewith Oedipus cursed his children:

Let them (for me) divide, both goods, yea rents and land:

With trenchant sword, and bloody blows, by force of mighty hand.

So cruel, hateful, and beastly is the nature of ambition and desire of rule.

Part Two

[Pyrrhus heard that Demetrius was sick, and decided to take advantage of the situation by making raids into Macedonia. The Epirotes found they had bitten off a bit more than they felt like chewing, as Demetrius (sick or not) gathered an army and pushed them back.]

Thus now, the peace concluded betwixt Demetrius and Pyrrhus, the other kings and princes began to find out Demetrius' intent, and why he had made so great preparation; and [they] being afraid thereof, wrote unto Pyrrhus by their ambassadors, that they wondered how he could let go **such opportunity and occasion**, and to tarry till Demetrius might with better leisure make wars upon him. And why he chose rather to **tarry and fight with him for the altars, temples, and sepulchres of the Molossians,** when he should be of greater power, and have no wars elsewhere to trouble him: than now that he [Pyrrhus] might easily drive him out of Macedon, having so many things in hand, and being troubled as he was in other places. And considering also that very lately he [Demetrius] had taken one of his [Pyrrhus'] wives from him, with the city of Corfu. For Lanassa misliking, that Pyrrhus loved his other wives better then her (they being of a barbarous nation), got her[self] unto Corfu: and desiring to marry some other king, sent for Demetrius, knowing that he of all other kings would soonest be won thereunto. Whereupon Demetrius went thither, and married her, and left a **garrison** in his city of Corfu.

Now these other kings that did advertise Pyrrhus in this sort, themselves did trouble Demetrius in the meanwhile: who **tracted time**, and yet went on with his preparation notwithstanding. For on the one side, Ptolemy entered Greece with a great army by sea, where he caused the cities to revolt against him. And Lysimachus on the other side also, entering into high Macedon by the country of Thracia [*Thrace*], burnt and spoiled all as he went. Pyrrhus also arming himself with them, went unto the city of **Berroea**, imagining (as afterwards it fell out) that Demetrius going against Lysimachus would leave all the low country of Macedon naked, without **garrison** or defense.

And the selfsame night that Pyrrhus departed, he imagined that

King Alexander the Great did call him, and that also he went unto him, and found him sick in his bed, of whom he had very good words and entertainment: insomuch as he promised to help him thoroughly. And Pyrrhus imagined also that he was so bold to demand of him again: "How (my Lord) can you help me, that lie sick in your bed?" and that Alexander made answer: "With my name only." And that moreover he suddenly therewithal got up on **his horse Nisea**, and rode before Pyrrhus to guide him the way.

Word Study

Counterfeit: This word came down from Latin, through Old French and then Middle English, using two roots that are still easy to pick out. The first, **counter**, means against, or in the wrong way; you may know the French word *contre* or the Italian *contra*. **Feit** comes from the verb *fere* which can mean either to copy or to make or do something. So something done falsely or in the wrong way is a **counterfeit**.

Narration and Discussion

Is knowledge of war the only subject that should interest princes and kings?

Why was Pyrrhus' response to his son seen later as a curse?

Discuss the value of (or danger of) using dreams as guidance.

Lesson Four

Introduction

This lesson could be titled "Easy Come, Easy Go," as Pyrrhus won the throne of Macedon (or part of it), and then lost it again. This who's in, who's out war seems like a game; although a game that causes "infinite sorrows and troubles" (**Lesson Five**), and which brings up the question of how it is played. Should rulers and those in authority be models of justice and equity? What happens when they demonstrate disloyalty, treason, and infidelity? (Is there any other way to win?)

Vocabulary

being a Macedonian king by nation: Lysimachus was a home-born Macedonian, and Demetrius was afraid that his Macedonian soldiers would "jump ship" out of patriotism.

set on by Pyrrhus: often "set on" means to attack, but in this case it means "placed there." These men were plants, sent to rouse support for Pyrrhus.

gave out: spread the word

required the watchword: demanded the password

oaken boughs: branches

refer all: surrender everything

to keep him from knowledge: to keep him from being recognized

avarice: greed

confines: boundaries

they are willingly together by the ears: other translations do not have this phrase, but keep the idea of being tied uncomfortably (and awkwardly) close together

he went to aid the Grecians against him: he went to the assistance of Athens, which had been besieged by Demetrius

suffered: allowed

greatly beholden unto them: very grateful, in their debt

requite: thank

to continue the Macedonians in war: keep them busy fighting (against someone else)

convoy of victuals: supply train

conductors: those bringing the supplies

rifled them wholly: ransacked them (see also **Word Study**)

letters and messengers: propaganda

had ever been their vassals and subjects: had served them

so feared Pyrrhus: alarmed him

confederates: allies; see **Word Study** for **Lesson Six**

People

Demetrius thus in the end being utterly overthrown in Syria: this is the last real mention of Demetrius. He surrendered to Seleucus, was taken prisoner, and died shortly afterwards in 284/283 B.C.

Historic Occasions

289 B.C.: the death of Agathocles, king of Sicily

288 B.C.: Lysimachus and Pyrrhus both invaded Macedonia

Reading

Part One

This vision he had in his dream, [was that] which made him bold, and furthermore encouraged him to go on with his enterprise. By which occasion, marching forward with all speed, in few days he ended his intended journey to the city of Berroea, which suddenly he took at his first coming to it: the most part of his army he laid in garrison there, the residue he sent away under the conduct of his captains, here and there, to conquer the cities thereabouts.

Demetrius having intelligence hereof, and hearing also an ill rumour that ran in his camp amongst the Macedonians, durst not lead them any further, for fear lest (when he should come near to Lysimachus, **being a Macedonian king by nation,** and a prince esteemed for a famous captain) they would shrink from him, and take Lysimachus' part: for this cause therefore he turned again upon the sudden against Pyrrhus, as against a strange prince, and ill beloved of the Macedonians.

But when he came to encamp near him, many coming from Berroea into his camp, blew abroad the praises of Pyrrhus, saying that he was a noble prince, invincible in wars, and one that courteously treated all those he took to his party: and amongst those, there were other[s] that were no natural Macedonians born, but **set on by Pyrrhus**, and feigned themselves to be Macedonians, who **gave out** that now occasion was offered to set them at liberty from Demetrius' proud and stately rule, and to take King Pyrrhus' part, that was a courteous prince, and one that loved soldiers and men of war. These words made the most part of Demetrius' army very doubtful, insomuch as the Macedonians looked about, to see if they could find out Pyrrhus to yield themselves unto him.

He had at that present left off his headpiece: by mean[s] whereof, perceiving he was not known, he put it on again, and then they knew him afar off, by sight of his goodly fair plume, and the goat's horns which he carried on the top of his crest. Whereupon there came a great number of Macedonians to his part, as unto their sovereign lord and king, and **required the watchword** of him. Other[s] put garlands of **oaken boughs** about their heads, because they saw his men crowned after that sort. And some were so bold also, as to go to Demetrius himself, and tell him, that in their opinions he should do very well and wisely to give place to fortune, and **refer all** unto Pyrrhus. Demetrius hereupon, seeing his camp in such uproar, was so amazed, that he knew not what way to take, but stole away secretly, disguised in a threadbare cloak, and a hood on his head **to keep him from knowledge**. Pyrrhus forthwith seized upon his camp, took all that he found, and was presently proclaimed in the field, King of Macedon.

Part Two

Lysimachus on the other side, came straight thither after him, and [said that] he had helped to chase Demetrius out of his realm, and therefore claimed half the kingdom with him [Pyrrhus]. Wherefore, Pyrrhus not trusting the Macedonians too far as yet, but rather standing in doubt of their faith, granted Lysimachus his desire, and thereupon divided all cities and provinces of the realm of Macedon between them. This partition was profitable for them both at that present, and stood then to good purpose, to pacify the war that otherwise might suddenly have risen between them.

But shortly after, they found that this partition was no end of their enmity, but rather a beginning of quarrel and dissension between them. For they whose **avarice** and insatiable greedy appetite, neither the sea, the mountains, [nor the] inhabitable deserts could contain, nor yet the **confines** that separate Asia from Europe determine: how should they be content with their own, without usurping others, when their frontiers join so near together, that nothing divides them? Sure it is not possible. For to say truly, **they are willingly together by the ears**, having these two cursed things rooted in them: that they continually seek occasion how to surprise each other, and either of them envies his neighbour's well doing. Howbeit in appearance they use these two terms, of peace and wars, as they do money: using it as they think good, not according to right and justice, but for their private profit. And truly they are men of far greater honesty, that make open war, and avow it: than those that disguise and colour the delay of their wicked purpose, by the holy name of justice or friendship.

Which Pyrrhus did truly then verify. For desiring to keep Demetrius down from rising another time, and that he should not revive again as [if he had] escaped from a long dangerous disease: **he went to aid the Grecians against him**, and was at Athens, where they **suffered** him to come into the castle and do sacrifice there unto the goddess Minerva. But coming out of the castle again the same day, he told the Athenians he was **greatly beholden unto them** for their courtesy, and the great trust they had reposed in him: wherefore to **requite** them again, he gave them counsel, never to **suffer** prince nor king from thenceforth to enter into their city, if they were wise, nor once open their gates unto them.

So, after that he made peace with Demetrius, who within short time being gone to make wars in Asia, Pyrrhus yet once again (persuaded thereunto by Lysimachus) caused all Thessaly to rise against him, and went himself to set upon those garrisons which **Demetrius** had left in the cities of Greece, liking better **to continue the Macedonians in war**, than to leave them in peace: besides that himself also was of such a nature, as could not long continue in peace.

Demetrius thus in the end being utterly overthrown in Syria, Lysimachus seeing himself free from fear on that side, and being at good leisure, as having nothing to trouble him otherwise: went straight to make war upon Pyrrhus, who then remained near unto the city of Edessa, and meeting by the way with the **convoy of victuals** coming towards him, [the army of Lysimachus] set upon the **conductors**, and **rifled them wholly**. By this means, first he [Lysimachus] distressed Pyrrhus for want of victuals: then he corrupted the princes of Macedon with **letters and messengers**, declaring unto them, what shame they sustained to have made a stranger their king (whose ancestors **had ever been their vassals and subjects**) and to have turned all those out of Macedon, that had been familiar friends of King Alexander the Great. Many of the Macedonians were won by these persuasions, which fact **so feared Pyrrhus**, that he departed out of Macedon with his men of war, the Epirotes, and other[s of] his **confederates:** and so lost Macedon by the selfsame means he won it.

Kings and princes therefore must not blame private men, though they change and alter sometime[s] for their profit: for therein they do but follow the example of princes, who teach them all disloyalty, treason, and infidelity, judging him most worthy of gain, that least observeth justice and equity.

Word Study

Rifle: What do **rifles** to shoot with have in common with **rifling** a drawer? **Rifle** gets its name from a Low German word meaning groove or furrow, which describes the grooves cut into **rifles**. The Old French word *rifler*, to ransack or plunder, gives us the other meaning of **rifle**. It means to scratch or strip something bare, which may not be all that different from making a groove.

Narration and Discussion

"Himself also was of such a nature, as could not long continue in peace." Is this an excuse for making war? You may also want to discuss this sentence: "Howbeit in appearance they use these two terms, of peace and wars, as they do money: using it as they think good, not according to right and justice, but for their private profit."

(Dryden: "they merely make use of those two words, peace and war, like current coin, to serve their occasions, not as justice but as expediency suggests.") (See Jeremiah 5:27-28; Jeremiah 22:17; Ecclesiastes 4:1; Galatians 5:15.)

"...they do but follow the example of princes, who teach them all disloyalty, treason, and infidelity, judging him most worthy of gain, that least observeth justice and equity." Is it true that common people tend to copy whatever their rulers do? Does that excuse them from responsibility for their own actions?

Lesson Five

Introduction

Pyrrhus had what should have been an eye-opening conversation with his advisor Cineas; but he did not act on that advice, and was soon off to war again. In this lesson we have the first mention of war elephants. Alexander the Great had popularized the use of elephants in battle, and it seems that Pyrrhus' success with them may have inspired the Carthaginians later on. (Hannibal of Carthage is still famous for his attempt to bring elephants over the Alps in 218 B.C.)

Vocabulary

ever entertained about him: kept as part of his court

trenchant: sharp, piercing

manifest of itself: obvious, clear

is hard adjoining it: is right next to it

more than: except for

letteth us now to be: what stops us now from being

happy state: a situation of security and well-being

footmen: foot soldiers

slings: soldiers using projectile weapons

benighted: forced to stop for the night

reserved: excepted

casting the peril every way: weighing the options (see also **Word Study**)

People

Tarentines: this is the first mention of the Tarentines, the people of **Tarentum**. Tarentum (now Taranto) is an important port city in southern Italy. (You can find it on the "heel" of Italy's "boot.")

Cineas Thessalian: "Thessalian" is where he came from, rather than an actual name

Demosthenes the orator: A statesman and orator (maker of public speeches) in ancient Athens (384–322 B.C.); he is the subject of Plutarch's *Life of Demosthenes*.

Agathocles: the "tyrant of Syracuse," king of Sicily, and father-in-law of Pyrrhus

Historic Occasions

282 B.C.: The Tarentines asked Pyrrhus to defend them against the Romans

281 B.C.: Seleucus defeated and killed Lysimachus in battle. In the same year, Ptolemy Keraunos, son of Ptolemy, murdered Seleucus and took the Macedonian throne.

Reading

Part One

So Pyrrhus being come home again to his kingdom of Epirus, forsaking Macedon altogether, fortune made him happy enough, and indeed he had good means to live peaceably at home, without any trouble, if he could have contented himself only with the sovereignty over his own natural subjects. But thinking, that if he did neither hurt other[s], nor that other[s] did hurt him, he could not tell how to spend his time, and by peace he should pine away for sorrow, as Homer said of Achilles:

He languished and pined by taking ease and rest:

And in the wars where travail was, he liked ever best.

And thus seeking matter of new trouble, fortune presented him this occasion. About this time, the Romans by chance made war with the **Tarentines**, who could neither bear their force, nor yet devise how to pacify the same, by reason of the rashness, folly, and wickedness of their governors, who persuaded them to make Pyrrhus their general, and to send for him for to conduct these wars: because he was less troubled at that time, than any of the other kings about them, and was esteemed of every man also to be a noble soldier, and famous captain.

[Omitted for length: a Tarentine named Meton warned the people that Pyrrhus would be a hard master rather than a friend, but he was ignored.]

The decree thus confirmed by voices of the people, they sent ambassadors into Epirus to carry presents unto King Pyrrhus, not only from the Tarentines, but from other Grecians also that dwelt in Italy, saying that they stood in need of a wise and skillful captain, that was reputed famous in martial discipline.

Part Two

There was in King Pyrrhus' court one **Cineas Thessalian**, a man of great understanding, and that had been **Demosthenes the orator's** scholar, who seemed to be the only man of all other in his time in common reputation, to be most eloquent, following the lively image and shadow of Demosthenes' passing eloquence. This Cineas, Pyrrhus **ever entertained about him,** and sent him ambassador to the people and cities thereabouts: where he verified Euripides' words:

As much as **trenchant** blades, in mighty hands may do.

So much can skill of eloquence, achieve and conquer too.

And therefore Pyrrhus would often say, that Cineas had won him more towns with his eloquence, than [he] himself had done by the sword: for which he did greatly honour and employ him in all his chief affairs.

Cineas perceiving that Pyrrhus was marvellously bent to these wars of Italy, finding him one day at leisure, discoursed with him in this sort: "It is reported, and it please your majesty, that the Romans are very good men of war, and that they command many valiant and warlike nations: if it please the gods we do overcome them, what benefit shall we have of that victory?"

Pyrrhus answered him again: "Thou dost ask me a question that is **manifest of itself**. For when we have once overcome the Romans, there can neither Grecian nor barbarous city in all the country withstand us, but we shall straight conquer all the rest of Italy with ease: whose greatness, wealth, and power, no man knoweth better than thyself."

Cineas, pausing a while, replied: "And when we have taken Italy, what shall we do then?"

Pyrrhus not finding his meaning yet, said unto him: "Sicilia as thou knowest, **is hard adjoining it**, and doth as it were offer itself unto us, and is a marvelous populous and rich land, and easy to be taken: for all the cities within the island are one against another, having no head that governs them, since **Agathocles** died, **more than** orators only that are their counsellors, who will soon be won."

"Indeed it is likely which your grace speaketh," quoth Cineas: "but when we have all in our hands: what shall we do in the end?"

Then Pyrrhus laughing, told him again: "We will then (good Cineas) be quiet, and take our ease, and make feasts every day, and be as merry one with another as we can possibl[y be]."

Cineas having brought him to that point, said again to him: "My Lord, what **letteth us now to be** quiet, and merry together, [if] we enjoy that presently without further travel and trouble, which we will now go seek for abroad, with such shedding of blood, and so **manifest** danger? and yet we know not whether ever we shall attain unto it, after we have both suffered, and caused other[s] to suffer infinite sorrows and troubles."

These last dangerous words of Cineas, did rather offend Pyrrhus, than make him think to alter his mind: for he was not ignorant of the

happy state he should thereby forego, yet could he not leave off the hope of that [which] he did so much desire.

So he sent Cineas before [him] unto the Tarentines, with three thousand **footmen**: and afterwards the Tarentines having sent him great store of flatbottoms, galleys, and of all sorts of passenger [vessels], he shipped into them twenty elephants, three thousand horsemen, and two and twenty thousand footmen, with five hundred bowmen and **slings**. All things thus ready, he [Pyrrhus] weighed anchors, and hoisted sails, and was no sooner in the main sea, but the north wind blew very roughly, out of season, and drave him to leeward. Notwithstanding, the ship which he was in himself, by great toil of the pilots and mariners turning to windward, and with much ado and marvellous danger recovered the coast of Italy. Howbeit the rest of his fleet were violently dispersed here and there, whereof some of them failing their course into Italy, were cast into the seas of Libya, and Sicilia. The other[s], not able to recover the point of Apulia, were **benighted**, and the sea being high wrought by violence cast them upon the shore, and against the rocks, and made shipwrecks of them.

The [royal galley] only [was] **reserved**, which through her strength, and the greatness of her burden, resisted the force of the sea that most violently beat against her. But afterwards, the wind turning and coming from the land, the sea cruelly raking over the height of her forecastle: in fine [it] brought her in **manifest** peril of opening, and splitting, and in danger to be driven from the coast, putting her out again to the mercy of the winds, which changed every hour. Wherefore Pyrrhus **casting the peril every way**, thought best to leap into the sea. After him forthwith leapt his guard, his servants, and other[s of] his familiar friends, venturing their lives to save him. But the darkness of the night, and rage of the waves (which the shore breaking, forced so to rebound back upon them) with the great noise also, did so hinder their swimming: that it was even day before they could recover any land, and yet was it by means that the wind fell.

As for Pyrrhus, he was so sea-beaten, and wearied with the waves, that he was able to do no more: though of himself he had so great a heart, and stout a courage, as was able to overcome any peril. Moreover, the Messapians (upon whose coast the storm had cast him) ran out to help him, and diligently laboured in all they could possible to save him, and received also certain of his ships that had

[e]scaped, in which were a few horsemen, about two thousand footmen, and two elephants.

With this small force, Pyrrhus marched on his journey to go by land unto Tarentum: and Cineas, being advertised of his coming, went with his men to meet him.

Word Study

Peril: danger or hazard. The Latin word *peri* means to try, as in ex-peri-ence, ex-peri-ment. Some experiments may put you in **peril**.

Narration and Discussion

"But thinking, that if he did neither hurt other[s], nor that other[s] did hurt him, he could not tell how to spend his time, and by peace he should pine away for sorrow..." (Dryden: "he who thought it a nauseous course of life not to be doing mischief to others, or receiving some from them...") Pyrrhus was dying of boredom! Should we feel sympathy? Would you have any suggestions for him?

Did Pyrrhus not understand what Cinea was saying, or did he understand it but reject it? Why could Pyrrhus not "leave off the hope of that [which] he did so much desire?" (How much is enough?)

Lesson Six

Introduction

Pyrrhus, with an enormous surge of ambition and confidence, took on the Roman army at Tarentum.

Vocabulary

> **they made their reckoning that Pyrrhus should fight for them:** they thought that the Epirotes would do all the work
>
> **places of show:** amusement places

pastime: hypothetically, without actually doing anything. Dryden says, "in their idle way, they fought their country's battles and conducted her campaigns in their talk."

feastings, mummeries, and such other like pleasures: "festivals, revels, and drinking parties"

musters: conscription; calling up men to serve in the war

puissant: powerful

arbitrament: arbitration; mediation

familiars about him: friends

prove their force: see what they can do

the whole aid of their confederates: their whole force (see also **Word Study**)

therewithal: about it

knew his pleasure: heard his orders

as yet out of order, and utterly unprovided: "as they were coming over, scattered and disordered"

passing rich glistering armour and furniture: one thing that set Pyrrhus apart from other men was his shining armour

withal: first use, "in addition"; second use, "with"

manifest: obvious

depended long in doubt: remained uncertain

People

Levinus the Roman consul: Publius Valerius Laevinus, commander of the Roman forces at the Battle of Heraclea. Two consuls were elected each year as leaders in Rome, and they were also expected to act as generals of the army.

Leonatus Macedonian: a Macedonian officer

Dionysius and **Hieronymus:** two historians, chroniclers of the time

35

Historic Occasions

280 B.C.: The Battle of Heraclea

Reading

Part One

Now when he was come to Tarentum, at the first he would do nothing by force, nor against the goodwill of the inhabitants: until such time as his ships that had escaped the dangers of the sea, were all arrived, and the greatest part of his army come together again.

But when he had all his army he looked for, seeing that the people of Tarentum could neither save themselves, nor be saved by any other, without straight order and compulsion, because **they made their reckoning that Pyrrhus should fight for them**, and in the meantime they would not stir out of their houses from bathing themselves, from banqueting, and making good cheer: first of all he caused all the parks and **places of show** to be shut up, where they were wont to walk and disport themselves in any kind of exercise, and as they walked, to talk of wars as it were **in pastime**, and to fight with words, but not to come to the blows. And further he forbade all **feastings, mummeries, and such other like pleasures**, as at that time were out of season. He trained them out also to exercise their weapons, and shewed himself very severe in **musters**, not pardoning any whose names were billed to serve in the wars: insomuch as there were many (which, unacquainted with such rough handling and government) forsook the city altogether, calling it a bondage, not to have liberty to live at their pleasure.

Furthermore, Pyrrhus having intelligence that **Levinus the Roman consul** came against him with a great **puissant** army, and that he was already entered into the land of Lucania, where he destroyed and spoiled all the country before him: albeit the Tarentines' aid of their confederates was not as yet come, he thought it a great shame to suffer his enemies' approach so near him, and therefore taking that small number he had, brought them into the field against Levinus. Howbeit he sent a herald before to the Romans, to understand of them, if (before they entered into this war) they could be content [that] the controversies they had with all the

Grecians dwelling in Italy, might be decided by justice, and therein [if they would] refer themselves to his **arbitrament**, who of himself would undertake the pacification of them. Whereunto the consul Levinus made answer, that the Romans would never allow him for a judge, neither did they fear him for an enemy.

Wherefore Pyrrhus going on still, came to lodge in the plain which is between the cities of Pandosia, and of Heraclea: and having news brought him that the Romans were encamped very near unto him on the other side of the river of Siris, he took his horse, and rode to the riverside to view their camp. So having thoroughly considered the form, the situation, and the order of the same, the manner of charging their watch, and all their fashions of doing: he wondered much thereat. And speaking to Megacles, one of his **familiars about him**, he said: "This order, Megacles" (quoth he), "though it be of barbarous people, yet is it not barbarously done, but we shall shortly **prove their force**."

After he had thus taken this view, he began to be more careful than he was before, and purposed to tarry till **the whole aid of their confederates** were come together, leaving men at the riverside of Siris, to keep the passage, if the enemies ventured to pass over, as they did indeed.

For they made haste to prevent the aid that Pyrrhus looked for, and passed their footmen over upon a bridge, and their horsemen at diverse fords of the river: insomuch as the Grecians fearing lest they should be compassed in behind, drew back. Pyrrhus [being] advertised thereof, and being a little troubled **therewithal**, commanded the captains of his footmen presently to put their bands in battle [ar]ray, and not to stir till they **knew his pleasure**: and he himself in the meantime marched on with three thousand horse[men], in hope to find the Romans by the riverside, **as yet out of order, and utterly unprovided**. But when he saw afar off a greater number of footmen with their targets ranged in battle, on this side [of] the river, and their horsemen marching towards him in very good order: he caused his men to join close together, and himself first began the charge, being easy to be known from other [men], if it had been no more but his **passing rich glistering armour and furniture**, and **withal**, for that his valiant deeds gave **manifest** proof of his well deserved fame and renown.

For, though he valiantly bestirred his hands and body both,

repulsing them he encountered **withal** in fight, yet he forgot not himself, nor neglected the judgement and foresight, which should never be wanting in a general of an army: but as though he had not fought at all, quietly and discreetly gave orders for everything, riding to and fro, to defend and encourage his men in those places, where he saw them in most distress.

Part Two

[Omitted for length: Pyrrhus had a violent encounter with an Italian soldier, and lost his horse.]

This mischance made King Pyrrhus look the better to himself afterwards, and seeing his horsemen give back, sent presently to hasten his footmen forward, whom he straight set in order of battle: and delivering his armour and cloak to one of his **familiars**, Megacles, and being hidden as it were in Megacles' armour, returned again to the battle against the Romans, who valiantly resisted him, so that the victory **depended long in doubt**. For it is said, that both the one side and the other did chase, and was chased, above seven times in that conflict.

The changing of the king's armour served very well for the safety of his own person, howbeit it was like to have marred all, and to have made him lose the field. For many of his enemies set upon Megacles, that wore the king's armour: and the party that slew him dead, and threw him stark to the ground, was one Dexius by name, who quickly snatched off his headpiece, took away his cloak, and ran to **Levinus the consul**, crying out aloud, that he had slain Pyrrhus, and withal shewed forth the spoils he supposed [himself] to have taken from him. Which being carried about through all the bands, and openly shewed from hand to hand, made the Romans marvellous joyful, and the Grecians to the contrary, both afeared and right sorrowful: until such time as Pyrrhus, hearing of it, went and passed alongst all **his bands** bareheaded, and barefaced, holding up his hand to his soldiers, and giving them to understand with his own voice, that it was himself.

Part Three

The elephants in the end were they indeed that won the battle, and did most distress the Romans: for, their horses seeing them afar off, were sore afraid, and durst not abide them, but carried their masters back in despite of them. Pyrrhus at the sight thereof, made his Thessalian horsemen to give a charge upon them whilst they were in this disorder, and that so lustily, as they made the Romans flee, and sustain great slaughter. For **Dionysius** writeth, that there died few less than fifteen thousand Romans at that battle. But **Hieronymus** speaketh only of seven thousand. And of Pyrrhus' side, **Dionysius** writeth, there were slain thirteen thousand. But **Hieronymus** sayeth less then four thousand: howbeit they were all of the best men of his army, and those whom most he trusted.

King Pyrrhus presently hereupon also took the Romans' camp, which they forsook, and won many of their cities from their alliance, spoiled, and overcame much of their country, [and in fact] he came within six and thirty miles of Rome itself. [Many of the Lucanians and Samnites came and joined him], whom he rebuked because they came too late to the battle. Howbeit a man might easily see in his face, that he was not a little glad and proud to have overthrown so great an army of the Romans with his own men and the aid of the Tarentines only.

Word Study

Confederate: to be **confederates** or a **confederacy** is to be joined by an agreement or treaty (or in a conspiracy) The Latin root *foedeus* means a treaty, and it is where we get our word **fidelity**. Those who make a treaty with (*con*) others are, therefore, con-feder-ates. To **con*spire*** means to *breathe* with someone.

Narration and Discussion

"For, though he valiantly bestirred his hands and body both, repulsing them he encountered withal in fight, yet he forgot not himself, nor neglected the judgement and foresight, which should never be wanting in a general of an army: but as though he had not fought at all, quietly and discreetly gave orders for everything, riding to and fro, to defend and encourage his men in those places, where he saw them in most distress." What lessons in leadership can we take from this example? (The Old Testament book of Nehemiah provides another instance of commanding-while-working, e.g. Nehemiah 5:15-16.)

"He was not a little glad and proud to have overthrown so great an army of the Romans with his own men, and the aid of the Tarentines only." How did Pyrrhus' army win the Battle of Heraclea? (Was it really just the elephants?)

Lesson Seven

Introduction

How would you negotiate peace with a Roman consul? Pyrrhus tried a unique version of "scare tactics."

Vocabulary

prove: confirm

bruit: noise

capitulations: concessions, conditions

abide: stand it any longer

vaunts: boasts

wherewith he was nothing able: with which he was not even able

treat of peace, treat for peace: talk about peace terms

touching: concerning

notwithstanding: however

hard by them: close to them

softly giving back: cautiously retreating

rehearsed the opinions...: spoke about Epicurean philosophy

felicity: great happiness (see **Word Study**)

hindereth the fruition: hinders the growth

"The gods grant that Pyrrhus and the Samnites were of such opinions, as long as they had wars against us": if the Epirotes were to follow Epicurean philosophy, the Romans would easily conquer them

magnanimity: generosity, greatness of spirit

took not in ill part: didn't seem to mind

upon his faith only: on his own word of honour

see their friends, and keep the feast of Saturn with them: Pyrrhus agreed to send the Roman prisoners of war back home temporarily (for the Saturnalia festival), and then they were to return to Epirus.

People

Molossians and Chaonians: tribes of Epirus

Caius Fabricius: Gaius Fabricius Luscinus/Lucinus Monocularis. He was elected consul in 282 B.C. and 278 B.C.

Appius Claudius Cæcus: a former consul and censor of Rome. There is an interesting chapter about him in *Famous Men of Rome*, by John H. Haaren and A.B. Poland.

Reading

Part One

On the other side, the Romans' hearts were so great, that they would not depose Levinus from his consulship, notwithstanding the loss he had received: and Caius Fabricius said openly, that they were not the Epirotes that had overcome the Romans, but Pyrrhus had overcome Levinus: meaning thereby, that this overthrow chanced unto them more through the subtlety and wise conduction of the general, than through the valiant feats and worthiness of his army. And hereupon they speedily supplied their legions again that were [di]minished, with other new soldiers in the dead men's place[s], and levied a fresh force besides, speaking bravely and fiercely of this war, like men whose hearts were nothing appalled.

Whereat Pyrrhus marvelling much, thought good first to send to the Romans, to prove if they would give any ear to an offer of peace, knowing right well that the winning of the city of Rome was no easy matter to compass, or attain, with that strength he presently had: and also that it would be greatly to his glory, if he could bring them to peace after this, his valiant victory.

Part Two

[Omitted for length: Pyrrhus sent Cineas to Rome, to try to negotiate an alliance. Things seemed to be going well, until Appius Claudius spoke up.]

But **Appius Claudius,** a famous man, who came no more to the Senate, nor dealt in matters of state at all by reason of his age, and partly because he was blind: when he understood of King Pyrrhus' offers, and of the common **bruit** that ran through the city, how the Senate were in mind to agree to the **capitulations** of peace propounded by Cineas, he could not **abide,** but caused his servants to carry him in his chair upon their arms unto the Senate door, his sons, and sons-in-law taking him in their arms, carried him so into the Senate house. The Senate made silence to honour the coming in of so notable and worthy a personage: and he, so soon as they had set him in his seat, began to speak in this sort:

"Hitherunto with great impatience (my Lords of Rome) have I borne the loss of my sight, but now, I would I were also as deaf as I am blind, that I might not (as I do) hear the report of your dishonourable consultations determined upon in Senate, which tend to subvert the glorious fame and reputation of Rome. What is now become of all your great and mighty brags you blazed abroad, through the whole world? that if Alexander the Great himself had come into Italy, in the time that our fathers had been in the flower of their age, and we in the prime of our youth, they would not have said everywhere that he was altogether invincible, as now at this present they do: but either he should have left his body slain here in battle, or at the least wise have been driven to flee, and by his death or flying should greatly have enlarged the renown and glory of Rome? You plainly show it now, that all these words spoken then, were but vain and arrogant vaunts of foolish pride. Considering that you tremble for fear of the Molossians and Chaonians, who were ever a prey to the Macedonians: and that ye are afraid of Pyrrhus also, who all his lifetime served and followed one of the guard unto Alexander the Great, and now is come to make wars in these parts, not to aid the Grecians inhabiting in Italy, but to flee from his enemies there about his own country, offering you to conquer all the rest of Italy with an army, **wherewith he was nothing able** to keep a small part of Macedon only for himself. And therefore you must not persuade yourselves, that in making peace with him, you shall thereby be rid of him: but rather shall you draw others to come and set upon you besides."

After that Appius had told this tale unto the Senate, everyone through the whole assembly desired rather war than peace. They dispatched Cineas away thereupon with this answer: that if Pyrrhus sought the Romans' friendship, he must first depart out of Italy, and then send unto them to **treat of peace**: but so long as he remained there with his army, the Romans would make wars upon him, with all the force and power they could make, yea although he had overthrown and slain ten thousand such captains as Levinus was.

Part Three

After this, there were sent ambassadors from Rome unto Pyrrhus, and amongst others, **Caius Fabricius, touching** the state of the prisoners. Cineas told the king, his master, that this Fabricius was one of the greatest men of account in all Rome, a right honest man, a good captain, and a very valiant man of his hands, yet poor indeed he was, **notwithstanding**. Pyrrhus taking him secretly aside, made very much of him, and amongst other things, offered him both gold and silver, praying him to take it, not for any dishonest respect he meant towards him, but only for a pledge of the goodwill and friendship that should be between them. Fabricius would [have] none of his gift: so Pyrrhus left him for that time.

Notwithstanding, the next morning, thinking to fear him, because he had never seen elephant[s] before, Pyrrhus commanded his men, that when they saw Fabricius and him talking together, they should bring one of his greatest elephants, and set him **hard by**

them, behind a hanging: which being done at a certain sign by Pyrrhus given, suddenly the hanging was pulled back, and the elephant with his trunk was over Fabricius' head, and gave a terrible and fearful cry. Fabricius **softly giving back**, nothing afraid, laughed and said to Pyrrhus, smiling: "Neither did your gold (oh king) yesterday move me, nor your elephant today fear me."

Furthermore, whilst they were at supper, falling in talk of diverse matters, specially **touching** the state of Greece, and the philosophers there: Cineas by chance spake of Epicurus, and **rehearsed the opinions of the Epicurians** touching the gods and government of the commonwealth, how they placed man's chief **felicity** in pleasure; how they fled from all office and public charge, as from a thing that **hindereth the fruition** of true **felicity**; how they maintained that the gods were immortal, neither moved with pity nor anger, and led an idle life full of all pleasures and delights, without taking any regard of men's doings.

But as he still continued this discourse, Fabricius cried out aloud, and said: **"The gods grant that Pyrrhus and the Samnites were of such opinions, as long as they had wars against us."**

Pyrrhus marvelling much at the constancy and **magnanimity** of this man, was more desirous [by] a great deal to have peace with the Romans, than before. And [he] privately prayed Fabricius very earnestly, that he would **treat for peace**, whereby he might afterwards come and remain with him, saying that he would give him the chief place of honour about him, amongst all his friends.

Whereunto Fabricius answered him softly: "That were not good (oh king) for yourself," quoth he: "for your men that presently do honour and esteem you, by experience if they once knew me, would rather choose me for their king, than yourself."

Such was Fabricius' talk, whose words Pyrrhus **took not in ill part**, neither was offended with them at all, as a tyrant would have been: but did himself report to his friends and familiars the noble mind he found in him, and delivered him **upon his faith only**, all the Roman prisoners: to the end that if the Senate would not agree unto peace, they might yet **see their friends, and keep the feast of Saturn with them**, and then to send them back again unto him. Which the Senate established by decree, upon pain of death to all such as should not perform the same accordingly.

[Omitted for length: Caius Fabricius and his co-consul did Pyrrhus a favour by uncovering a plot by his own physician to poison him. In thanks, Pyrrhus sent home their prisoners of war (seemingly without conditions). But the Romans preferred not to owe any favours to an enemy who refused to leave Italy, and so they sent the same number of prisoners back to the Epirotes.]

Word Study

Felicity: this word for happiness has been passed down from the Latin word *felix,* "happy." Those familiar with French or Spanish will recognize the root word in phrases such as "Félicitations" (congratulations) and "Feliz cumpleaños" (happy birthday).

Narration and Discussion

"Whereat Pyrrhus marvelling much, thought good first to send to the Romans, to prove if they would give any ear to an offer of peace, knowing right well that the winning of the city of Rome was no easy matter to compass, or attain, with that strength he presently had: and also that it would be greatly to his glory, if he could bring them to peace after this, his valiant victory." Why did Pyrrhus think that now might be a good time to negotiate peace with Rome?

The speech of Appius Claudius is the earliest recorded example of a political speech in Latin. How did it change the mood of the Roman Senate?

Lesson Eight

video: carl Linnaeus's systema Naturae

Introduction

"And furthermore, for peace and his friendship, they would give no ear to it, before the wars were ended, and that he had sent away his army again by sea, into the kingdom of Epirus." Pyrrhus had two choices: go home peacefully, or fight the Roman army.

Vocabulary

marvellous ill: terrible

turnings and places of retire: the advantages (to them) of the uneven ground

in the plain field: on even ground

pressed in upon their enemies' pikes with their swords: Pyrrhus' army was fighting in the Macedonian phalanx formation, moving as a body and holding their spears (pikes) out in front

and their troubles thereby yet nothing eased: not gaining any advantage by dying

severed: stopped fighting

carriage: baggage

both the one and the other did retire: they both backed off

began to wax cold: they were beginning to lose interest in this war

even at a clap: all at once

sundry: different, separate

as if both enterprises had been already in his hand: Pyrrhus assumed that he would win whichever of the two he took on

to attain to the greater matters: to attempt even bigger stakes, such as attacking Carthage

make his way: prepare things

they should not choose but tarry his occasion: his aid to them was at his convenience, not theirs

he drave the Carthaginians before him: he routed them

martial men, and given to arms: military men, trained fighters

Mare Libycum: part of the Mediterranean Sea, along the coast of Libya and extending eastward as far as Crete

did set him aloft: gave him an inflated sense of power and importance

when he would press them…: Pyrrhus needed more men and money, and he began to "squeeze" the Sicilians too hard for assistance

compelled: forced (see **Word Study**)

People

Carthaginians: this is the first mention here of the Carthaginians. Carthage was a powerful city in North Africa, and a longtime enemy of Rome. Dryden's translation calls them "the Phoenicians."

Ptolemy surnamed the lightning: Ptolemy Keraunos or Ceraunus, the son of Ptolemy Soter (see **Lesson One**) was king of Macedon from 281 B.C. to 279 B.C.. Keraunos is Greek for "Thunderbolt."

Gauls: the "barbarian" tribes of Northern Europe (a very general definition, but sufficient for this story)

Mamertines: a pirate colony, founded by former mercenary soldiers

Historic Occasions

279 B.C.: the Battle of Asculum (the "Pyrrhic victory"). In the same year, a large number of Gauls came to Macedon, fought with (and killed) Ptolemy, and continued to invade other parts of Greece.

278 B.C.: A successful Greek defense at Thermopylae and Delphi, against the Gauls. Pyrrhus transferred his army to Sicily.

277 B.C.: Pyrrhus captured the city of Eryx. Fighting between the Greeks and the Gauls, including the Battle of Lysimachia; Antigonus reclaimed Macedon.

276 B.C.: Pyrrhus demanded resources from Sicily, which made him very unpopular.

Reading

Part One

Wherefore Pyrrhus seeing no remedy, but that he must needs fight another battle, after he had somewhat refreshed his army, [they] drew towards the city of Asculum, where he fought the second time with the Romans: and was brought into a **marvellous ill** ground for horsemen, by a very swift running river, from whence came many brooks and deep marshes, insomuch as his elephants could have no space nor ground to join with the battle of the footmen, by reason whereof there was a great number of men hurt and slain on both sides. *[After many were wounded and killed, night put an end to the engagement.]*

But the next morning, Pyrrhus [caused a detachment to possess themselves of those incommodious grounds, and, mixing slingers and archers among the elephants, with full strength and courage, he advanced in a close and well-ordered body.] The Romans, missing the other day's **turnings and places of retire**, were now compelled to fight all on a front **in the plain field**: and striving to break into the battle of Pyrrhus' footmen before the elephants came, they desperately **pressed in upon their enemies' pikes with their swords,** not caring for their own persons what became of them, but only looked to kill and destroy their enemies. [After a long and obstinate fight, the first giving ground is reported to have been where Pyrrhus himself engaged with extraordinary courage; but the Romans were carried away by the overwhelming force of the elephants, not being able to make use of their valour, but overthrown as it were by the eruption of a sea or an earthquake], rather than tarry to be trodden under feet, and overthrown by them, whom they were not able to hurt again, but be by them most grievously martyred, **and their troubles thereby yet nothing eased**.

The chase was not long, because they fled but into their camp: and Hieronymus the historiographer writeth, that there died six thousand men of the Romans, and of Pyrrhus' part about three thousand five hundred and five, as the king's own chronicles do witness. Nevertheless, Dionysius makes no mention of two battles given near unto the city of Asculum, nor that the Romans were certainly overthrown: howbeit he confirmeth that there was one battle only that continued until sunset, and that they scarcely **severed** also when night was come on, Pyrrhus being hurt on the arm with a spear, and his **carriage** robbed and spoiled by the Samnites besides. And further, that there died in this battle, above fifteen thousand men, as well of Pyrrhus' side, as of the Romans' part: and that at the last, **both the one and the other did retire**. And some say that it was at that time Pyrrhus answered one, who rejoiced with him for the victory they had won: "If we win another of the price," quoth he, "we are utterly undone."

For indeed then had he lost the most part of his army he brought with him out of his realm, and all his friends and captains, [and there were no others there to make recruits], and [he] perceived also that the confederates he had in Italy, **began to wax cold**. Where[as] the Romans to the contrary, did easily renew their army with fresh soldiers, which they caused to come from Rome as need required, (much like unto a lively spring, the head whereof they had at home in their country), and they fainted not at all for any losses they received, but rather were they so much the more hotly bent, stoutly determining to abide out the wars, whatever betide.

Part Two

And thus whilst Pyrrhus was troubled in this sort, new hopes, and new enterprises were offered unto him, that made him doubtful what to do. For **even at a clap** came ambassadors to him out of Sicilia, offering to put into his hands the cities of Syracuse, of Agrigentum, and of the Leontines, and beseeching him to aid them to drive the **Carthaginians** out of the isle, thereby to deliver them from all the tyrants. And on the other side also, news was brought him from Greece, how **Ptolemy surnamed the lightning**, was slain, and all his army overthrown in battle against the **Gauls**, and that now he should come in good hour for the Macedonians, who lacked but a king. Then he cursed his hard fortune that presented him all at once, such **sundry** occasions to do great things: and **as if both enterprises had been already in his hand**, he made his account that of necessity he must lose one of them. So, long debating the matter with himself, which of the two ways he should conclude upon: in the end he resolved, that by the wars of Sicilia, there was good mean[s] **to attain to the greater matters**, considering that Africa was not far from them. Wherefore, disposing himself that way, he sent Cineas thither immediately to **make his way**, and to speak to the towns and cities of the country as he was wont to do: and in the meantime left a strong garrison in the city of Tarentum, to keep it at his devotion, wherewith the Tarentines were very angry. For they made request unto him, either to remain in their country to maintain wars with them against the Romans (which was their meaning why they sent for him), or else if he would needs go, at the least wise to leave their city in as good state as he found it. But he answered them again very roughly, that **they should not choose but tarry his occasion**.

And with this answer [he] took ship, and sailed towards Sicilia: where so soon as he was arrived, he found all that he hoped for, for the cities did willingly put themselves into his hands. And where necessity of battle was offered him to employ his army, nothing at the beginning could stand before him. For, with thirty thousand footmen, two thousand five hundred horsemen, and two hundred sail which he brought with him, **he drave the Carthaginians before him**, and conquered all the country under their obedience.

[Omitted for length: Pyrrhus also captured the city of Eryx.]

Part Three

There dwelt a barbarous people at that time about Messina, called the **Mamertines**, who did much hurt to the Grecians thereabouts, making many of them pay tax and tribute: for they were a great number of them, and all men of war and good soldiers, and had their name also of Mars, because they were **martial men, and given to arms**. Pyrrhus led his army against them, and overthrew them in battle: and put their collectors to death, that did levy and exact the tax, and razed many of their fortresses. And when the Carthaginians required peace and his friendship, offering him ships and money, pretending greater matters: he made them a short answer, that there was but one way to make peace and love between them, to forsake Sicilia altogether, and to be contented to make **Mare Libycum** the border betwixt Greece and them. For his good fortune, and the force he had in his hands, **did set him aloft**, and further allured him to follow the hope that brought him into Sicilia, aspiring first of all unto the conquest of Libya.

Now, to pass him over thither, he had ships enough, but he lacked rowers and mariners: wherefore **when he would press them, then he began to deal roughly with the cities of Sicilia**, and in anger **compelled**, and severely punished, them that would not obey his commandment. This he did not [do] at his first coming, but contrarily had won all their good wills, speaking more courteously to them than any other did, and shewing that he trusted them altogether, and troubled them in nothing. But suddenly being altered from a popular prince, unto a violent tyrant, he was not only thought cruel and rigorous, but that worst of all is, unfaithful and ungrateful: nevertheless, though they received great hurt by him, yet they suffered it, and granted him any needful thing he did demand.

Word Study

Compel: In Latin, *pellere* is to push, strike, or drive something, and the word was passed down to us through Anglo-French. To **compel** is to push or force someone, and it implies the use of actual force. To **impel** means almost the same thing, but it does not usually involve physical force. *Pellere* is also the root of our word "pulse."

Narration and Discussion

Was Pyrrhus' treatment of the Sicilians any different from the way the Mamertine "pirates" operated?

Why was being "unfaithful and ungrateful" worse than "cruel and rigorous?"

Lesson Nine

Introduction

Pyrrhus' up-and-down fortune now seemed to take a turn for the worse. After wearing out his welcome in Sicily, he tried to defend Tarentum against the Romans. But the Romans were getting stronger all the time, and "trusting more to his good fortune, than any good reason might move him" didn't seem to be enough.

Vocabulary

all things fell out against Pyrrhus: things started to go against him

did again some of them confederate with the Carthaginians: some of them conspired against him with the Carthaginians

to cloak his flying, to colour his departing: to give him a good excuse to leave

the very strait itself of Messina: the strait between Sicily and the mainland

durst not present him battle: dared not attack

tarried: waited for

straits: narrow passages

his rearward: the rear guard

his vanguard: those at the front

incontinently: without hesitation

the voward: the vanguard, the front ranks

his strength: his stronghold, place of safety

casteth well: makes good throws

only to make a foray, and to get some spoil in the country: Dryden says Pyrrhus wanted "merely to plunder and waste the country."

diverse holds: several towns

he marched against King Antigonus: this is the Battle of the Aous

strait: narrow

environed: surrounded

they would not once base their pikes: they would not raise their weapons

redound to: reflect (see also **Word Study**)

People

Manius Curius: Manius Curius Dentatus, a Roman consul

Antigonus: Antigonus II Gonatus; see note in the introduction

Historic Occasions

275 B.C: the Battle of Beneventum

274 B.C.: the Battle of the Aous

Reading

Part One

Then **all things fell out against Pyrrhus**, not one after another, nor by little and little, but all together at one instant, and all the cities generally hated him to the death, and **did again some of them confederate with the Carthaginians**, and others with the Mamertines, to set upon him. But when all Sicilia was thus bent against him, he received letters from the Samnites and Tarentines, by which they advertised him, how they had much ado to defend themselves within their cities and strongholds, and that they were wholly driven out of the field: wherefore they earnestly besought him speedily to come to their aid. This news came happily to him, **to cloak his flying**, that he might say it was not for despair of good success in Sicilia that he went his way: but true it was indeed, that when he saw he could no longer keep it, than a ship could stand still among the waves, he sought some honest shadow **to colour his departing**. And that surely was the cause why he returned again into Italy.

Nevertheless, at his departure out of Sicily, they say that looking back upon the isle, he said to those that were about him: "O what a goodly field for a battle, my friends, do we leave to the Romans and Carthaginians, to fight the one with the other?" And verily so it fell out shortly after, as he had spoken.

Part Two

But the barbarous people conspiring together against Pyrrhus, the Carthaginians on the one side, watching his passage, gave him battle on the sea, in **the very strait itself of Messina**, where he lost many of his ships, and fled with the rest, and took the coast of Italy. And there the Mamertines on the other side, being gone thither before, to the number of eighteen thousand fighting men: **durst not present him battle** in open field, but **tarried** for him in certain **straits** of the mountains, and in very hard places, and so set upon **his rearward**, and disordered all his army. They slew two of his elephants, and cut off a great number of **his rearward**, so he was compelled himself in person to come from **his vanguard**, to help them. *[Omitted for length: Pyrrhus fought with all his might against the "barbarous people."]* After that, they let him go, and troubled him no more.

Pyrrhus holding on his journey, arrived at length in the city of Tarentum *[see **Lessons Five** and **Six**]*, with twenty thousand footmen, and three thousand horse. And with these (joining thereto the choicest picked men of the Tarentines) he went **incontinently** into the field to seek out the Romans, who had their camp within the territories of the Samnites, which were then in very hard state.

For their hearts were killed, because that in many battles and encounters with the Romans, they were ever overthrown. They were very angry besides with Pyrrhus, for that he had forsaken them, to go his voyage unto Sicilia, by reason whereof there came no great number of soldiers into his camp. But notwithstanding, he divided all his strength into two parts, whereof he sent the one part into Lucania, to occupy one of the Roman consuls that was there, to the end he should not come to aid his companion; and with the other part he went himself against **Manius Curius**, who lay in a very strong place of advantage near to the city of Benevento, attending the aid that should come to him out of Lucania, besides also that the soothsayers (by the signs and tokens of the birds and sacrifices) did counsel him not to stir from thence.

Pyrrhus, to the contrary, desiring to fight with **Manius** before his aid came unto him, which he [Manius] looked for out of Lucania, took with him the best soldiers he had in all his army, and the warlikest elephants, and marched away in the night, supposing to steal upon Manius on the sudden, and give an assault unto his camp.

Now Pyrrhus having a long way to go, and through a woody country, his lights and torches failed him, by reason whereof many of his soldiers lost their way, and they lost a great deal of time also, before they could again be gathered together: so as in this space the night was spent, and the day once broken, the enemies perceived plainly how he came down the hills. This at the first sight made them [the Romans] muse a while, and put them in a little fear: nevertheless Manius having had the signs of the sacrifices favourable, and seeing that occasion did press him to it, went out into the field, and set upon **the voward** of his enemies, and made them turn their backs. [This put the whole army into such consternation] that there were slain a great number of them in the field, and certain elephants also taken.

This victory made Manius Curius leave **his strength**, and come into the plain field, where he set his men in battle [ar]ray, and overthrew his enemies by plain force on the one side: but on the other he was repulsed by violence of the elephants, and compelled to draw back into his own camp, wherein he had left a great number of men to guard it. So when he saw them upon the ramparts of his camp all armed, ready to fight, he called them out, and they coming fresh out of places of advantage to charge upon the elephants, compelled them in a very short time to turn their backs, and flee through their own men, whom they put to great trouble, and disorder: so as in the end, the whole victory fell upon the Romans' side, and consequently by means of that victory, followed the greatness and power of their Empire. For the Romans being grown more courageous by this battle, and having increased their force, and won the reputation of men unconquerable: immediately after, [they] conquered all Italy besides, and soon after that, all Sicilia.

Part Three

To this end as you see, came King Pyrrhus' vain hope he had to conquer Italy and Sicilia, after he had spent six years continually in wars, during which time his good fortune decayed, and his army consumed. Notwithstanding, his noble courage remained always invincible, what losses soever he had sustained: and moreover whilst he lived, he was ever esteemed the chiefest of all the kings and princes in his time, as well for his experience and sufficiency in wars, as also for the valiantness and hardiness of his person. But what he won by famous deeds, he lost by vain hopes: desiring so earnestly that which he had not, as he forgot to keep that which he had. Wherefore **Antigonus** compared him unto a dice player that **casteth well**, but cannot use his luck.

[Pyrrhus and his remaining troops returned to Epirus.]

Now having brought back again with him, into Epirus, eight thousand footmen, and five hundred horsemen, and being without money to pay them, he devised with himself to seek out some new war to entertain those soldiers, and keep them together. [Some of the Gauls joining him], he entered into the realm of Macedon (which **Antigonus**, Demetrius' son, held at that time) with intent **only to make a foray, and to get some spoil in the country**. But when he saw that he had taken **diverse holds**, and moreover, that two thousand men of war of the country came and yielded themselves unto him: he began to hope of better success, than at the first he looked for.

For upon that hope he **marched against King Antigonus** [him]self, whom he met in a very **strait** valley, and at his first coming, gave such a lusty charge upon his rearward, that he put all Antigonus' army in great disorder. For Antigonus had placed the **Gauls** in the rearward of his army to close it in, which were a convenient number, and [they] did valiantly defend the first charge: and the skirmish was so hot, that the most of them were slain.

After them, the leaders of the elephants, perceiving they were **environed** on every side, yielded themselves and their beasts. Pyrrhus seeing his power to be now increased with such a supply, trusting more to his good fortune, than any good reason might move him, thrust further into the battle of the Macedonians, who were all afraid, and troubled for the overthrow of their rearward, so as **they would not once base their pikes**, nor fight against him. He for his part holding up his hand, and calling the captains of the bands by their names, straightways made all the footmen of Antigonus turn wholly to his side: who, flying, saved himself with a few horsemen, and kept certain of the cities in his realm upon the sea coast.

But Pyrrhus in all his prosperity, judging nothing more to **redound to** his honour and glory than the overthrow of the Gauls, laid aside their goodliest and richest spoils, and offered up the same in the temple of Minerva Itonida, with an inscription. Immediately after this battle, all the cities of the realm of Macedon yielded unto him.

Word Study

Redound: to reflect an action (in the same way as throwing a pebble in water creates waves), or to cause a particular result. **Redound** comes from the Latin *redundare*, to overflow, which contains the word *undare*, to surge; it comes from *unda*, wave, which is where we get words like "undulate" and "redundant."

Narration and Discussion

"O what a goodly field for a battle, my friends, do we leave to the Romans and Carthaginians, to fight the one with the other?" Plutarch called these words prophetic. What did he mean? (Hint: look up the Punic Wars.)

What did Plutarch say was the real outcome of the Roman victory at the Battle of Beneventum?

Lesson Ten

Introduction

Pyrrhus thought it would be an easy job to besiege and invade Sparta; especially with twenty-five thousand foot soldiers, two thousand more on horseback, and twenty-four elephants. But he didn't count on the Spartans.

Vocabulary

Æges: the first capital of Macedon, where Alexander the Great was proclaimed king. It is now called Vergina.

hardly: roughly, severely

insolency: insolence; disrespect (see **Word Study**)

a mad man to go apparelled in purple like a king: saying that he might as well take off his crown now, because he was finished

procure him: negotiate with him

Laconia, Lacedaemonia: both refer to the region of southern Greece (the **Peloponnesus**) around the city of Sparta. Spartans were often called Lacedaemonians.

forthwith: without delay

which Antigonus kept in bondage: which were under the rule of Macedon

after the Laconian manner: in the disciplined style of the Spartans.

feigning: pretending

abusing: pretending, deceiving

for that he made wars upon them in such sort: because he was attacking them in that manner

ill provided: poorly equipped (armed)

that they made no reckoning to assault it hotly: that they did not attempt to attack the city quickly and violently

cast a trench: dig a trench

to the end that: with the goal that

stay the elephants: obstruct the passage of the elephants

to go in hand withal: to get to work

felicity: great happiness (also in Lesson Seven)

magnanimity: Dryden simplifies this to "falling as became Spartans," but that seems to miss the implication of **magnanimity**, which could be defined here as "heart" or "spirit."

tarry his coming: delay him

did let the soldiers also to fight steadily in order of battle: "Let" here means prevented; the soldiers kept slipping on the soft ground.

essayed: tried, attempted

People

Cleonymus, King of Sparta: he was a younger son of the previous king, and was passed over in favour of his nephew **Areus I**

Areus: see note about **Cleonymus. Areus I** was king of Sparta from 309-265 B.C. He was succeeded by his son **Acrotatus II**.

Archidamia: a wealthy Spartan queen

Historic Occasions

272 B.C.: Pyrrhus led an invasion of **Laconia** (*see vocabulary note*) and laid siege to Sparta, with the supposed plan that he would put **Cleonymus** in power.

Reading

Part One

But when he had the city of **Æges** in his power, he used the inhabitants thereof very **hardly**, and specially because he left a great garrison of the Gauls there which he had in pay. This nation is extreme[ly] covetous, as then they shewed themselves: for they spared not to break up the tombs wherein the kings of Macedon lay buried there, took away all the gold and silver they could find, and afterwards with great **insolency** cast out their bones into the open wind.

Pyrrhus was told of it, but he lightly passed it over, and made no reckoning of it: either because he deferred it till another time, by reason of the wars he had then in hand: or else for that he durst not meddle with punishing of these barbarous people at that time. But whatsoever the matter was, the Macedonians were very angry with Pyrrhus, and blamed him greatly for it. Furthermore, having not yet made all things sure in Macedon, nor being fully possessed of the same: [new hopes and projects] came into his head, and mocking Antigonus, [Pyrrhus] said he was **a mad man to go apparelled in purple like a king**, when a poor cloak might become him like a private man.

Now, **Cleonymus, King of Sparta,** being come to **procure him** to bring his army into the country of **Lacedaemon,** Pyrrhus was very willing to it. *[Omitted for length: details about Cleonymus, who badly wanted revenge against the current rulers of Sparta.]*

Hereupon he [Cleonymus] brought him [Pyrrhus] into Lacedaemonia **forthwith,** with five and twenty thousand footmen, two thousand horse, and four and twenty elephants: by which preparation, though by nothing else, the world might plainly see, that Pyrrhus came with a mind not to restore **Cleonymus** again unto Sparta, but of intent to conquer for himself (if he could) all the country of **Peloponnesus.** For in words he denied it to the Lacedaemonians themselves, who sent ambassadors unto him when he was in the city of Megalipolis, where he told them that he was come into **Peloponnesus,** to set the towns and cities at liberty **which Antigonus kept in bondage:** and that his true intent and meaning was to send his young sons into Sparta (so they [the Spartans] would be contented) to the end they might be trained **after the Laconian manner,** and from their youth have this advantage above all other kings, to have been well brought up.

But **feigning** these things, and **abusing** those that came to meet him on his way, they took no heed of him, till he came within the coast of **Laconia,** into the which he was no sooner entered, but he began to spoil and waste the whole country. And when the ambassadors of Sparta reproved and found fault with him, **for that he made wars upon them in such sort,** before he had openly proclaimed it: he made them answer: "No more have you yourselves used to proclaim that, which you purposed to do to others." Then one of the ambassadors, called Mandricidas, replied again unto him in the Laconian tongue: "If thou be a god, thou wilt do us no hurt, because we have not offended thee: and if thou be a man, thou shalt meet with another that shall be better than thyself."

Then he marched directly to Sparta, where Cleonymus gave him counsel, even at the first, to assault it. But he would not so do, fearing (as they said) that if he did it by night, his soldiers would sack the city: and said it should be time enough to assault it the next day at broad daylight, because there were but few men within the town, and beside[s], they were very **ill provided.** And furthermore, King Areus himself was not there, but [had] gone into Creta [Crete] to aid the

Gortynians, who had wars in their own country. And doubtless, that only was the saving of Sparta from taking, **that they made no reckoning to assault it hotly**: because they thought it was not able to make resistance.

Part Two

For Pyrrhus camped before the town, thoroughly persuaded with himself, that he should find none to fight with him: and Cleonymus' friends and servants also did prepare his lodging there, as if Pyrrhus should have come to supper to him, and lodged with him.

When night was come, the **Lacedaemonians** counselled together, and secretly determined to send away their wives and little children into Creta. But the women themselves were against it, and there was one among them called **Archidamia**, who went into the Senate house with a sword in her hand, to speak unto them in the name of all the rest, and said that they did their wives great wrong, if they thought them so fainthearted as to live after Sparta were destroyed. Afterwards it was agreed in council, that they should **cast a trench** before the enemies' camp, and that at both the ends of the same they should bury carts in the ground unto the midst of the wheels, **to the end that** being fast set in the ground, they should **stay the elephants**, and keep them from passing further.

And when they began **to go in hand withal**, there came wives and maids unto them, some of them their clothes girt up round about them, and others all in their smocks, to work at this trench with the old men, advising the young men that should fight the next morning, to rest themselves in the meanwhile. So the women took the third part of the trench to task, which was six cubits broad, four cubits deep, and eight hundred foot long, as Philarchus sayeth: or little less as Hieronymus writeth.

Then when the break of day appeared, and the enemies removed to come to the assault: the women themselves fetched the weapons which they put into the young men's hands, and delivered them the task of the trench ready made, which they before had undertaken, praying them valiantly to keep and defend it, telling them withal, how great a pleasure it is to overcome the enemies, fighting in view and sight of their native country, and what great **felicity** and honour it is to die in the arms of his mother and wife, after he hath fought valiantly like an honest man, and worthy of the **magnanimity** of Sparta.

Part Three

Now Pyrrhus marched in person with his battle of footmen, against the front of the Spartans, who being a great number also, did **tarry his coming** on the other side of the trench: the which, besides that it was very ill to pass over, **did let the soldiers also to fight steadily in order of battle**, because the earth being newly cast up, did yield under their feet.

Wherefore, Ptolemy, King Pyrrhus' son, passing all alongst the trench side with two thousand Gauls, and all the choice men of the Chaonians, **essayed** if he could get over to the other side at one of the ends of the trench where the carts were: which being set very deep into the ground, and one joined unto another, they did not only hinder the assailants, but the defendants also. Howbeit in the end, the Gauls began to pluck off the wheels off these carts, and to draw them into the river.

But **Acrotatus, King Areus'** son, a young man, seeing the danger, ran through the city with a troop of three hundred lusty youths besides, and went to enclose Ptolemy behind before he espied him, for that he passed a secret hollow way till he came even to give the charge upon them: whereby they were enforced to turn their faces towards him, one running in another's neck, and so in great disorder were thrust into the trenches, and under the carts: insomuch as at the last, with much ado, and great bloodshed, **Acrotatus** and his company drave them back, and repulsed them.

In the end, the battle having continued all the day long, the night did separate them.

Word Study

Insolency, Insolence: This word that usually means "disrespectful" or "rude" actually has a milder meaning. The Latin word *solere* means to be accustomed, so to be in-*solent* means to depart from custom, to do something unusual. **Insolent** was first used in English to mean someone arrogant or haughty; later (in the 17th century) it came to mean someone who did not show proper respect for authority.

Breaking up the tombs of the kings would probably qualify as both.

Narration and Discussion

How did Pyrrhus misjudge the ease of taking Sparta?

What part did the women play in defending the city? Do you think Spartan women were "unfeminine?"

Lesson Eleven

Introduction

After the siege of Sparta, Pyrrhus and his army were called to help resolve a dispute in the city of Argos (in which the Macedonian king Antigonus was supposed to be supporting the other side). Their mission was derailed by a Spartan ambush. Although Pyrrhus was still determined to enter Argos and support his friend, others in the city sent pleas to the Epirotes and the Spartans to keep their fighting outside the walls. The Spartans agreed, but Pyrrhus made no promises.

Vocabulary

to let them: to prevent them

broil: brawl

the press: the crowd, the ranks

upon the hanging of a steep hill: Dryden translates this "on slippery and steep ground," which would seem to make more sense since Pyrrhus was actually still in the trench.

retire: setback

in their rooms: in place of the women and old men

new supplies: additional forces

stomach: desire, appetite

he won nothing but blows: he won nothing but losses

gave over: gave up

spoil: plunder

to lie there in garrison: keep his troops there

a sedition: a feud

Argos: a rival city of Sparta. Its people were the **Argives**.

whose nature and disposition was such...: who was always ambitious for more

straitest: narrowest

notwithstanding: in spite of the fact

asunder: apart

lighting off: jumping off

considering that the wars against them were ended: the war had already been ended; this was an "unofficial" attack

to honour his funerals: to honour his loss

neuter: neutral territory

no caution nor sufficient pledge to perform it: Pyrrhus sent no hostage as proof that he would not attack Argos, so his promise was not completely trusted.

People

Aminias Phocian: Ameinias the Phocian, a commander in the service of Antigonus.

Areus: the king of Sparta; see note in **Lesson Ten**

Antigonus: the son of Demetrius. See note in the introduction.

Evalcus, Oraesus: Eualcus, Oroissus

64

Historic Occasions

272 B.C.: The siege of Sparta continued

Reading

Part One

At the break of day, Pyrrhus led his army unto the assault. On the other side also, the Lacedaemonians with a marvellous courage and magnanimity, far greater then their force, bestirred themselves wonderfully to make resistance, having their wives by them that gave them their weapons wherewith they fought, and were ready at hand to give meat and drink to them that needed, and did also withdraw those that were hurt to cure them. The Macedonians likewise for their part, endeavoured themselves with all their might to fill up the trench with wood and other things, which they cast upon the dead bodies and armours, lying in the bottom of the ditch: and the Lacedaemonians again, laboured all that they could possible **to let them**.

But in this great **broil**, one perceived Pyrrhus a-horseback to have leapt the trench, passed over the strength of the carts, and made force to enter into the city. Wherefore those that were appointed to defend that part of the trench, cried out straight: and the women fell a-shrieking, and running, as if all had been lost.

And as Pyrrhus passed further, striking down with his own hands all that stood before him, a Cretan shot at him, and struck Pyrrhus in his horse through both sides: who leaping out of **the press** for pain of his wound, dying, carried Pyrrhus away, and threw him **upon the hanging of a steep hill**, where he was in great danger to fall from the top. This put all his servants and friends about him in a marvellous fear, and therewithal the Lacedaemonians seeing them in this fear and trouble ran immediately unto that place, and with force of shot drave them all out of the trench.

After this **retire**, Pyrrhus caused all assault to cease, hoping the Lacedaemonians in the end would yield, considering there were many of them slain in the two days past, and all the rest in manner hurt. Howbeit, the good fortune of the city (whether it were to prove the valiantness of the inhabitants themselves, or at the least to shew what power they were of even in their greatest need and distress, when the Lacedaemonians had small hope left) brought one **Aminias Phocian** from Corinth, one of King Antigonus' captains with a great band of men, and put them into the city to aid them: and straight after him, as soon as he had entered, **King Areus** arrived also on the other side from Creta, and two thousand soldiers with him.

So the women went home to their houses, making their reckoning that they should not need any more to trouble themselves with wars. They gave the old men liberty also to go and rest themselves, who being past all age to fight, for necessity's sake yet were driven to arm themselves, and take weapon[s] in hand: and in order of battle placed the new-come soldiers **in their rooms.**

Part Two

Pyrrhus, understanding that **new supplies** were come, grew to greater **stomach** than before, and enforced all that he could, to win the town by assault. But in the end, when to his cost he found that **he won nothing but blows,** he **gave over** the siege, and went to **spoil** all the country about, determining **to lie there in garrison** all the winter.

He could not for all this avoid his destiny. For there rose **a sedition** in the city of **Argos** between two of the chiefest citizens, Aristeas and Aristippus: and because Aristeas thought that **King Antigonus** did favour his enemy Aristippus, he made haste to send first unto Pyrrhus, **whose nature and disposition was such, that he did continually heap hope upon hope, ever taking the present prosperity, for an occasion to hope after greater to come.** And if it fell out he was a loser, then he sought to recover himself, and to restore his loss, by some other new attempts. So that neither for being conqueror, nor overcome, he would ever be quiet, but always troubled some[one], and himself also: by reason whereof, he suddenly departed towards **Argos.**

But **King Areus**, having laid ambushes for him in diverse places, and occupied also the **straitest** and hardest passages, by the which he was to pass; he [**Areus**] gave a charge upon the Gauls and Molossians, which were in the tail of his [Pyrrhus'] army.

The fray was very hot about Ptolemy, Pyrrhus' son, for they were all the chief men of the Lacedaemonians with whom he had to do, led by a valiant captain called **Evalcus**. But as he fought valiantly against those that stood before him, there was a soldier of Creta called **Oraesus**, born in the city of Aptera, a man very ready of his hand, and light of foot, who running alongst by him, strake him [Ptolemy] such a blow on his side, that he fell down dead in the place.

Prince Ptolemy being slain, his company began straight to flee: and the Lacedaemonians followed the chase so hotly, that they took no heed of themselves, until they saw they were in the plain field far from their footmen. Wherefore, Pyrrhus unto whom the death of his son was newly reported, being afire with sorrow and passion, turned suddenly upon them, with the men of arms of the Molossians, and being the first that came unto them, made a marvellous slaughter among them. For, **notwithstanding** that everywhere before that time he was terrible and invincible, having his sword in his hand: yet then he did shew more proof of his valiantness, strength, and courage, then he had ever done before.

[On his riding his horse up to Evalcus], Evalcus turned on the toe side, and gave Pyrrhus such a blow with his sword, that he missed little the cutting off his bridle hand: for he cut indeed all the reins of the bridle **asunder**. But Pyrrhus straight ran him through the body with his spear, and **lighting off** from his horse, he put all the troop of the Lacedaemonians to the sword that were about the body of Evalcus, being all chosen men. Thus the ambition of the captains was [the] cause of that loss unto their country for nothing, **considering that the wars against them were ended**.

Part Three

But Pyrrhus having now, as it were, made sacrifice of these poor bodies of the Lacedaemonians for the soul of his dead son, and fought thus wonderfully also **to honour his funerals**, converting a great part of his sorrow for his death into anger and wrath against the enemies: he afterwards held on his way directly towards Argos.

And understanding that **King Antigonus** had already seized the hills that were over the valley, he lodged near unto the city of Nauplia: and the next morning following sent a herald unto Antigonus, and gave him defiance, calling him wicked man, and challenged him to come down into the valley to fight with him, to try which of the two should be king. Antigonus made him answer, that he made wars as much with time, as with weapon[s]: and furthermore, that if Pyrrhus were weary of his life, he had ways open enough to put himself to death.

The citizens of Argos also sent ambassadors unto them both, to pray them to depart, since they knew that there was nothing for them to see in the city of Argos, and that they would let it be a **neuter**, and friend unto them both. King Antigonus agreed unto it, and gave them his son for hostage. Pyrrhus also made them fair promise to do so too, but because he gave **no caution nor sufficient pledge to perform it**, they mistrusted him the more.

Word Study

Broil or brawl: To be **embroiled** in a **brawl** comes from the Middle English word *broylen*, to present in disorder, or quarrel; but that word goes back to the Old French *broiller*, to jumble together. Another word with a similar meaning, **melee** (*mêlée*), comes from roots that give us **mingle, melange,** and **mixture.** We also use **mix** and **mix it up** to mean fighting with fists, which is what might happen if you **mingle** in a **melee.**

Narration and Discussion

"Antigonus made him answer, that he made wars as much with time, as with weapon[s]..." What did he mean by that?

Pyrrhus, fighting in the field after the death of his son, "did shew more proof of his valiantness, strength, and courage, then he had ever done before." Considering the many risks Pyrrhus had taken in his lifetime, how was it possible for him to now show more strength and courage?

Lesson Twelve

Introduction

The end of the story describes Pyrrhus' arrival by night at Argos, and an almost comic scene of trying to get a herd of elephants unloaded and reloaded in the dark. When Pyrrhus started the next day by coming across a sculpture that seemed like a bad omen, he was ready to call the whole thing off. But getting all the elephants back outside the city walls turned out to be harder than getting them in.

Vocabulary

put in: sent in

possessed: seized, took over

towers: also called turrets; raised platforms on the backs of the elephants, from which arrows could be fired

in tumult: in confusion

perceived it: figured out what was going on

without: outside

his son: Alcyoneus (see note below)

thought best to retire: thought they should retreat

straitness: narrowness

overthrow a piece of the wall: break down some of the wall so they could enlarge the gate

reported his message quite contrary: the messenger got it backwards; he told **Helenus** to bring more soldiers in, instead of preparing to help those coming out

giving back: trying to retreat

yet they that were behind, and did still thrust forward into the press, did not permit them: some of the soldiers were still coming in as others were trying to get out

overthwart: across

ware: wore

familiars: friends

set upon: attacked

an Argian born: a citizen of Argos

what he was: who he was

straight blown abroad amongst diverse: immediately spread everywhere

used him: treated him

apparelled him in good sort: gave him better clothes

with honourable convoy: with an escort. Dryden says, "restored him to his kingdom of Epirus," which is a bit different from simply "sent him home." Helenus was not the next king in any case; Alexander II succeeded his father as king of Epirus.

People

Aristeas: one of the citizens of Argos involved in the dispute, and the one who asked Pyrrhus for help

Antigonus: the king of Sparta

Helenus: the youngest son of Pyrrhus

Alcyoneus: a son of Antigonus (and grandson of Demetrius). This does not appear to be the son (Demetrius II Aetolicus) who eventually succeeded Antigonus, since this later Demetrius was born in 276/275 B.C.

Historic Occasions

272 B.C.: the attack on Argos

Reading

Part One

Pyrrhus then coming hard to the walls of Argos in the night, and finding one of the gates called Diamperes, opened by **Aristeas,** he

put in his Gauls: who **possessed** the marketplace, before the citizens knew anything of it.

But because the gate was too low to pass the elephants through with their **towers** upon their backs, they [the Gauls] were driven to take them off, and afterwards when they were within, to put them on in the dark, and **in tumult**: by reason whereof they lost much time, so that the citizens in the end **perceived it**, and ran incontinently unto the castle of Aspides, and into other strong places of the city.

And therewithal, they sent with present speed unto **Antigonus**, to pray him to come and help them, and so he did: and after he was come hard to the walls, he remained **without** with the scouts, and in the meantime sent **his son** with his chiefest captains into the town, who brought a great number of good soldiers and men of war with them.

At the same time also arrived **Areus**, king of Sparta, with a thousand of the Cretans, and most lusty Spartans: all which joining together, came to give a charge upon the Gauls that were in the marketplace, who put them in a marvellous fear and hazard.

[Omitted for length: the Gauls had some trouble finding their way around town in the dark, and decided to wait for daylight before doing anything else. When Pyrrhus entered the marketplace at dawn, the sight of a sculpture that seemed to be a bad omen disturbed him.]

Pyrrhus being half discouraged with the sight of [this], and also because nothing fell out well according to his expectation, **thought best to retire**; but fearing the **straitness** of the gates of the city, he sent [a message] unto his son **Helenus**, whom he had left **without** the city with the greatest part of his force and army, commanding him to **overthrow a piece of the wall** that his men might the more readily get out, and that he might receive them, if their enemies by chance did hinder their coming out.

Part Two

But the messenger whom he sent, was so hasty and fearful, with the tumult that troubled him in going out, that he did not well understand what Pyrrhus said unto him, but **reported his message quite contrary**. Whereupon the young Prince Helenus taking the best soldiers he had with him, and the rest of his elephants, entered into the city to help his father, who was now **giving back**: and so long as he had room to fight at ease, retiring still, he valiantly repulsed those that set upon him, turning his face oft unto them. But when he was driven unto the street that went from the marketplace to the gate of the city, he was kept in with his own men that entered at the same gate to help him. But they could not hear when Pyrrhus cried out, and bade them go back, the noise was so great: and though the first had heard him, and would have gone back, **yet they that were behind, and did still thrust forward into the press, did not permit them**.

Besides this moreover, the biggest of all the elephants by misfortune fell down **overthwart** the gate, where he grinding his teeth did hinder those also, that would have come out and given back. Furthermore, another of the elephants that were entered before the city, called Nico ("conquering"), seeking his governor that was stricken down to the ground from his back with terrible blows, ran upon them that came back upon him, overthrowing friends and foes one in another's neck, till at the length having found the body of his master slain, he lift[ed] him up from the ground with his trunk, and carrying him upon his two [tusks], returned back with great fury, treading all under feet he found in his way.

Thus every man being thronged and crowded up together in this sort, there was not one that could help himself: for it seemed to be a mass and heap of a multitude, and one whole body shut together, which sometime[s] thrust forward, and sometime[s] gave back, as the sway went. They fought not so much against their enemies, who set upon them behind: but they did themselves more hurt, than their enemies did. For if any drew out his sword, or based his pike, he could neither scabbard the one again, nor lift up the other, but thrust it full upon his own fellows that came in to help them, and so killed themselves, one thrusting upon another.

Wherefore Pyrrhus seeing his people thus troubled and harried to and fro, took his crown from his head, which he **ware** upon his helmet, that made him known of his men afar off, and gave it unto one of his **familiars** that was next unto him: and trusting then to the goodness of his horse, flew upon his enemies that followed him.

It fortuned that one hurt him with a pike, but the wound was neither dangerous nor great: wherefore Pyrrhus **set upon** him that had hurt him, who was **an Argian born**, a man of mean condition, and a poor old woman's son, whose mother at that present time was gotten up to the top of the tiles of a house, as all other women of the city were, to see the fight. And she, perceiving that it was her son whom Pyrrhus came upon, was so affrighted to see him in that danger, that she took a tile, and with both her hands cast it upon Pyrrhus.

The tile falling off from his head by reason of his headpiece, lighted full in the nape of his neck, and brake his neckbone asunder: wherewith he was suddenly so benumbed, that he lost his sight with the blow, the reins of his bridle fell out of his hand, and himself fell from his horse to the ground, by Licymmias' tomb, before any man knew **what he was**, at the least the common people. Until at the last there came one Zopyrus, that was in pay with Antigonus, and two or three other soldiers also that ran straight to the place, and knowing him, dragged his body into a gate, even as he was coming again to himself out of this trance. This Zopyrus drew out a Slavon sword he wore by his side, to strike off his head *[and did so with some difficulty]*.

Part Three

The matter was **straight blown abroad amongst diverse**: whereupon **Alcyoneus** running thither, asked for the head that he might know it again. But when he had it, he ran presently unto his father withal, and found him talking with his familiar friends, and cast Pyrrhus' head before him. Antigonus looking upon it, when he knew it, laid upon his son with his staff, and called him cruel murderer, and unnatural barbarous beast: and so hiding his eyes with his cloak, wept for pity, (remembering the fortune of his grandfather Antigonus, and of his father Demetrius) and then caused Pyrrhus' head and body to be honourably burnt and buried.

Afterwards **Alcyoneus** meeting **Helenus** (King Pyrrhus' son) in very poor state, muffled up with a poor short cloak: **used him** very courteously with gentle words, and brought him to his father. Antigonus seeing his son bringing of him, said unto him: "This part now (my son) is better then the first, and pleaseth me a great deal more. But yet thou hast not done all thou shouldst: for thou shouldst have taken from him his beggarly cloak he weareth, which doth more shame us that are the gainers, than him that is the loser."

After he had spoken these words, Antigonus embraced Helenus, and having **apparelled him in good sort**, sent him home **with honourable convoy** into his realm of Epirus. Furthermore, all Pyrrhus' camp and army [having fallen into his hands], he courteously received all his friends and servants.

Narration and Discussion

Discuss this: "But yet thou hast not done all thou shouldst: for thou shouldst have taken from him his beggarly cloak he weareth, which doth more shame us that are the gainers, than him that is the loser."

What was the strongest point of Pyrrhus' character? What was the weakest?

Nicias
(ca. 470 B.C. – 413 B.C.)

The Golden Age of Athens

The strongest world power during the fifth century B.C. was the Persian Empire. By the time Nicias was born, Persia had overcome most of its rivals; but the Greeks held out, and they were entering a "Golden Age," particularly in the city-state of Athens.

The Athenian "Golden Age" is also called the "Age of Pericles," after its leader **Pericles**, who lived from 495-429 B.C. and was a chief influence in the city from about 461 B.C. until his death.

What was a *strategos*?

The word that North translates "captain" is the Greek word *strategos*. It means a military general, but the *strategoi* were also governors in Athens. The Athenians elected ten *strategoi* each year.

Who was Nicias?

What we know of Nicias' early life comes mostly from Plutarch: he was a man who had inherited wealth; he was by nature generous and pious, although not particularly sociable; and he seemed to be the natural leader of the aristocratic party after the death of Pericles.

What is "timorous?"

Plutarch describes Nicias as **timorous**. This word comes from the Latin *timor*, meaning "fear." It usually signifies someone who is timid or nervous, lacking confidence; or, more positively, it could mean "humble" or "cautious." The theme of Nicias' **timorousness**, and how it affects his leadership, is something to watch throughout the story.

Who was Cleon?

Cleon was the main political opponent of Nicias until his death in 422 B.C. Although he was an aristocrat himself, he represented the interests of the commercial class, a lower tier of citizens.

Who was Alcibiades?

Alcibiades (450-404 B.C.) is the subject of a *Life* by Plutarch. After the death of Cleon, he became the political rival of Nicias (although, on occasions such as a threatened ostracism, they did co-operate). The Sicilian Expedition (the subject of the last half of the *Life of Nicias*) was taken on at his urging.

What was the Peloponnesian War?

The half-century of peace after the Persian War ended with the outbreak of the Peloponnesian War in 431 B.C. The Peloponnesus is the southern region of Greece, the location of Sparta (Lacedaemon); and the war was a struggle for power between Athens and Sparta. The fighting was occasionally halted by agreements such as the Peace of Nicias in 421; but the war dragged on until the year 404, ten years after Nicias' death. This *Life* begins with events after the death of Pericles, soon after the war began.

Lesson One

Introduction

We may not have childhood stories of Nicias, but there are many resources for learning about Athenian life during the time he was growing up. It is not hard to imagine the things that Nicias might have seen: the Parthenon, built between 447-438 B.C.; Phidias' statue of Zeus at Olympia, finished around 435 B.C. and one of the Seven Wonders of the World; the first performances of plays by Aeschylus, Sophocles, and Euripides. The philosopher Socrates was born the same year as Nicias, and died only a few years before him.

As a politician, Nicias felt he had only one real asset in persuading people to follow him: his money. He didn't have the strong personality of either Pericles or Cleon; but he did have the financial means to sponsor public events and religious processions. He could also stage-manage a performance, as we see in the story of the spectacle at Delos.

Vocabulary

clerkly: in a scholarly or learned manner; "clerically"

things that are past all challenge and correcting: Dryden translates this "works of inimitable excellence." Plutarch is referring here to histories written by others, not the actual people studied.

the communalty: the state, commonwealth

withal: in addition

to advance and prefer him: to give him more power

feeding their humour with gain: pleasing them with gifts

timorous: see introductory note

liberality, with charges...: by providing entertainment and public events at his own expense

the profits of the same: the income from that land

giving out abroad: telling everyone

about Laurion side: around Mount Laurium

People

Thucydides: There are two people named Thucydides mentioned here. One is the historian Thucydides, author of *The History of the Peloponnesian War*; the other is a politician, the political rival of Pericles. Plutarch also names **Philistus**, another historian.

Reading

Part One

In my fancy, the ambition and contention to write or to speak more **clerkly** than others, sheweth always a base envious mind, like a scholar full of his school points. But when it striveth with **things that are past all challenge and correcting**, then is it extreme folly and madness. Since therefore I may not pass over nor omit certain things which **Thucydides and Philistus** have already set down; and especially those wherein they lay open Nicias' nature and qualities, which the variety of his successes and fortune did cover: I must lightly touch them, and report so much as is necessary, and convenient, lest men condemn me for sloth and negligence. And in the rest I have endeavoured to gather and propound things not commonly marked and known, which I have collected as well out of sundry men's works and ancient records, as out of many old antiquities: and of them all compiled a narration, which will serve (I doubt not) to decipher the man and his nature.

Of Nicias therefore [it] may be said that which Aristotle hath written of him: that there were three famous citizens of Athens, very honest men, and which favored **the communalty** with a natural fatherly love: Nicias the son of Niceratus; **Thucydides** [the politician], the son of Milesius; and Theramenes the son of Agnon. But of the three, this last was of smallest account: for he is flouted as a foreigner. Of the other two, **Thucydides**, being the elder, did many good acts in favour of the nobility against Pericles, who always took part with the inferior sort.

Nicias, that was the younger, had reasonable estimation in Pericles' lifetime: for he was joined captain with him, and oftentimes also had charge by himself alone without him. After Pericles' death, the nobility raised him to great authority, to be as a strong bulwark for them against Cleon's insolency and boldness: and **withal**, he had the love of the people, **to advance and prefer him**.

Now this Cleon in truth could do much with the people, he did so flatter and dandle them, like an old man, still **feeding their humour with gain**: but yet they themselves whom he thus flattered, knowing his extreme covetousness, impudency, and boldness, preferred Nicias before him, because his gravity was not severe nor odious, but mingled with a kind of modesty, that he seemed to fear the presence of the people, which made them thereby the more to love and esteem him. For being (as he was) of a fearful and mistrustful nature and disposition: in wars he cloaked his fear with good fortune, which ever favoured him alike in all his journeys and exploits that he took in hand where he was captain. Now being much afraid of accusers, this **timorous** manner of his [in civil life] was found to be popular, whereby he won him[self] the goodwill of the people: and by means thereof rose daily more and more, the people [being fearful of all that despised them, but willing to promote one who seemed to be afraid of them]. For the greatest honour nobility can do to the people, the **communalty**, is to show that they do not despise them.

Now Pericles, who through his perfect virtue only, and [the] force of his great eloquence, ruled the whole state and commonwealth of Athens, he need[ed] no counterfeit colour, nor artificial flattering of the people, to win their favour and goodwill: but Nicias lacking that, and having wealth enough, sought thereby to creep into the people's favour. And where Cleon would entertain the Athenians [by amusing them with bold jests]: Nicias finding himself no fit man to work by such encounter, crept into the people's favour with **liberality, with charges of common plays, and with suchlike sumptuousness**, exceeding in cost and pleasant sports, not only all those that had been before him, but such also as were in his time.

Part Two

Men write also of certain sumptuous and devout acts [that Nicias] did in the isle of Delos, where the dancers and singers which the cities of

Greece sent thither to sing rhymes and verses in the honour of Apollo were wont before to arrive disorderly: and the cause was, for the numbers of people that ran to see them, who made them sing straight without any order, and landing in haste out of their ships, they left their apparel, and put on such vestments as they should wear in procession, and their garlands of flowers on their heads, all at one present time.

But Nicias, being commanded to go thither to present the singers of Athens, landed first in the isle of Renia, hard adjoining to the isle of Delos, with his singers, his beasts for sacrifice, and with all the rest of his train, carrying a bridge with him, which he had caused to be made at Athens, upon measure taken of the channel betwixt the one and the other isle, [magnificently adorned with gilding and colouring, and with garlands and tapestries]: which in the night he set up upon the channel, being not very broad; and the next morning by break of the day [he] caused his singers to pass over upon it, singing all the way as they went, in his procession so nobly set forth, even unto the very temple of Apollo.

And when the sacrifice, the feast, and games that were to be played were finished, he gave a goodly palm tree of copper, which he offered up to Apollo, bought lands besides that cost him ten thousand drachmas, which he consecrated also unto [the god of the isle], and ordained, that **the profits of the same** should be yearly bestowed by the Delians, upon an open sacrifice and feast, in the which they should pray to their god for the health and prosperity of Nicias: and so caused it to be written and graven upon a pillar he left in Delos, as a perpetual monument and keeper of his offering, and foundation. Afterwards, this copper palm tree being broken by winds, it fell upon the great image of the Naxians' gift, and threw it down to the ground.

Surely in this ceremony and act of his, there was a marvellous pomp, and great shew of popular ambition: nevertheless, he that shall consider of [Nicias'] life and actions, may easily persuade himself that above all he did it of very pure zeal and devotion, and secondly, to give pleasure and pastime to the people. For by Thucydides' report of him, he was one that feared the gods with trembling, and was wholly given to religion. We find written in one of the dialogues of Pasiphoon, that Nicias did sacrifice daily to the gods, and kept a soothsayer continually in his house, **giving out abroad** that it was to counsel with him what should happen about the affairs of the commonwealth: but in truth it was to inquire of his own business, and specially of his mines of silver.

For he had many great mines **about Laurion side**, that were very profitable to him: but **withal** they [were] digged with great danger, and he was driven continually to keep a marvellous number of slaves at work there. The most part of Nicias' riches was in ready money, and thereby he had many cravers and hangers on him, whom he gave money unto: for he gave as well unto wicked people that might do mischief, as unto them that deserved reward, and were worthy of his liberality. Thus was his fear a rent to the wicked, as his liberality was also a revenue to the good.

Discussion and Narration

"Now this Cleon in truth could do much with the people, he did so flatter and dandle them, like an old man, still feeding their humour with gain." How did Nicias win their confidence in his own way?

What used to be the problem with the religious processions at Delos? How did Nicias solve this?

Lesson Two

Introduction

Nicias noticed that men who were envied usually ended up in trouble; so he made sure everyone heard him thanking the gods for every success. He also avoided taking part in anything risky, because he didn't want to be blamed if things went wrong. But even cautious Nicias could occasionally produce a surprise.

Vocabulary

would suffer no access unto him: would allow no one to see him

in his hot house to wash him: bathing and grooming himself

looked like nobody: looked terrible

abate: lessen

offices: duties

ought: anything

the plague: in 430-429 B.C., there was a horrendous epidemic in Athens, which was the cause of Pericles' death

Laconia: the region of Sparta

Reading

Part One

Now Nicias, being thus timorous of nature, and fearing to give any little occasion to the orators to accuse him, kept himself so warily that he neither durst eat nor drink with any man in the city, nor yet put forth himself in company to talk, or pass the time amongst them, but altogether avoided such sports and pleasures.

For when he was in office, he would never [come] out of the council house, but still busied himself in dispatching causes, from morning till night, and was ever the first that came, and last that went away. And when he had no matter of state in hand, then was he very hardly to be spoken withal, and **would suffer no access unto him**, but kept close in his house: and some of his friends did ever answer [people] that came to his gate, and prayed them to pardon him, saying that he was busy then about affairs of the commonwealth.

One Hieron, whom Nicias had brought up in his house, and had himself taught him both learning and music, was his greatest procurer and instrument to keep him from speech with any man, and brought him to this reputation of greatness and gravity. This Hieron did serve his turn, and helped him secretly to inquire what he would understand of the soothsayers, and gave out these words among the people: that Nicias led too miserable and painful a life, for the overgreat care he took to serve the commonwealth: insomuch, as though he were **in his hot house to wash him**, or at his table at meat, his mind ran still of some matters about the commonwealth, and to serve the state, did neglect his own private affairs: so that he scant began to sleep and take rest, when others commonly had slept their first sleep, and that **he looked like nobody**. Furthermore, that he was grown crabbed and uncourteous, even to such as before had been his familiar friends. So that, said he, he loseth them together with his goods, and all for service of the commonwealth: where others grow rich, and win friends, by the credit they have to be heard of the people, and can make merry among them, and sport with the matters of state which they have in their hands.

Now in truth, such was Nicias' life that he might truly say that which Agamemnon spake of himself in the tragedy of *Euripides*:

In outward show of stately pomp all others I exceed,

And yet the people's underling I am in very deed.

Part Two

[Nicias observed that the people, in the case of men of eloquence, or of eminent parts, made use of their talents upon occasion, but were always jealous of their abilities, and held a watchful eye upon them, taking all opportunities to humble their pride and **abate** their reputation; as was manifest in their condemnation of Pericles, their banishment of Damon, their distrust of Antiphon the Rhamnusian, but especially in the case of Paches who took Lesbos; who, having to give an account of his conduct, in the very court of justice, unsheathed his sword and slew himself.] Nicias, I say, remembering these examples, sought ever to flee from these **offices** which were either too great, or too small; and when he accepted any, had special regard to work surely, and to venture nothing. Whereby all his enterprises that he took in hand, as we may easily conjecture, prospered marvellous well: but yet he imputed nothing to his own wisdom, nor yet to his virtue and sufficiency, but thanked fortune ever for all, and praying diligently to the gods, contented himself to lessen his glory, and that only to avoid envy. As the event of things falling out even in his time do sufficiently witness unto us.

Part Three

For the city of Athens having sustained many great losses and overthrows, he was never a party, nor had **ought** to do, in any of them. As once for example: the Athenians were overcome in Thracia by the Chalcidonians, howbeit it was under the leading of Calliades and Xenophon, who were their captains. Another time, the loss they had in Ætolia under the charge of Demosthenes. Moreover at Delium, a city of Boeotia, where they lost a thousand men at one conflict, Hippocrates then being their general. And as touching **the plague**, the greatest number laid the fault thereof to Pericles, who by reason of wars kept the men that came out of the country, within the walls of the city of Athens: and so by changing of air, and their wonted manner of life, they fell into it. Now with none of all these great troubles and misfortunes, was Nicias ever burdened: but contrariwise he being captain took the isle of Cythera, which the Lacedaemonians inhabited, being an excellent place for situation to molest and destroy the country of **Laconia**. He won divers cities again that had rebelled in Thracia, and brought them once more under the obedience of Athens. At his first coming, having shut in the Megarians within their walls, he took the isle of Minoa: and at his departure thence, shortly after won the haven of Nisea also.

[Making a descent upon the Corinthian territory, he fought a successful battle, and slew a great number of the Corinthians with their captain, Lycophron. There it happened that two of his men were left, by an oversight, when they carried off the dead; which, when he understood, he stopped the fleet, and sent a herald to the enemy for leave to carry off the dead; though by law and custom, he that by a truce craved leave to carry off the dead was hereby supposed to give up all claim to the victory. Nor was it lawful for him that did this to erect a trophy, for his is the victory who is master of the field, and he is not master who asks leave, as wanting power to take.] Nicias, notwithstanding, was contented rather to forsake the honour of his victory, than to leave the bodies of two of his countrymen in the field without burial.

Narration and Discussion

How did Hieron excuse Nicias' unwillingness to see visitors? Was the excuse true? Some Scriptures to consider: Mark 10:44; Matt. 6:17.

Explain the choice that Nicias made after the battle with the Corinthians (in the last paragraph of the reading).

Lesson Three

Introduction

Some enemy soldiers were stranded on an island, and the obvious plan was to besiege them and take them prisoner. However, capturing them proved difficult, and the Athenians, led by Nicias' enemy Cleon, began to wonder loudly why this simple maneuver was taking so long, or why they didn't agree to a recent peace proposal by the Lacedaemonians. "Were I general," Cleon said, "they should not hold out so long." Nicias decided that the best response was to challenge him to do a better job.

Vocabulary

fetch a marvellous compass: go a long way around

victuals: food, supplies

burdened: blamed

importunate: persistent

licentiousness: unruly behaviour

fatness and lustiness: richness

noisome: poisonous

broil: turmoil

husbandmen: landowners and farmers

hearken: give attention

Historic Occasions

423 B.C.: The Battle of Amphipolis

Reading

Part One

And when the Peloponnesians had prepared great armies both by sea and by land to besiege the fort of Pyle [*Pylos*], the which Demosthenes the captain had fortified: battle being given by sea, it chanced there remained four hundred natural citizens of Sparta, within the isle of Spacteria [*Sphacteria*].

Now the Athenians thought it a noble exploit of them, (as indeed it was) to take those four hundred alive: howbeit the siege was very sore, because they lacked water even in the midst of summer, and were forced to **fetch a marvellous compass** to bring **victuals** to their camp, which when winter should be once come would be very dangerous, and almost an impossible thing to do. Whereupon, they then became sorry, and repented them much that they had sent away the ambassadors of the Lacedaemonians, which came to them to treat of peace, and that they had (through Cleon's procurement) suffered them to depart in that sort without resolution taken. [Cleon opposed it chiefly out of a pique to Nicias; for, being his enemy, and observing him to be extremely solicitous to support the offers of the Lacedaemonians, he persuaded the people to refuse them.]

But when the people saw that this siege drew out in length, and that their camp suffered grievous wants and necessities: then fell they out with Cleon, and he again **burdened** Nicias, saying that through his fear he would let the besieged Spartans escape, and that if he [Cleon] had been captain, they should not have holden out so long. Thereupon the Athenians said aloud to Cleon: "And why dost not thou go thither yet to take them?"

Moreover Nicias [him]self also rising up, openly gave him his authority to take this Pyle, and bade him levy as many soldiers as he would to go thither, and not to brag with such impudent words where was no danger, but to do some notable service to the commonwealth.

Cleon at the first shrank back, being amazed withal, little thinking they would have taken him so suddenly at his word. But in the end, perceiving the people urged him to it, and that Nicias also was **importunate** with him: ambition so inflamed him, that he not only took the charge upon him, but in a bravery said that within twenty days after his departure he would either put all the Spartans to the sword, or bring them prisoners unto Athens. The Athenians, hearing Cleon say so, had more [inclination] to laugh [at] than to believe that [which] he spake: for it was their manner ever to laugh at his anger and folly.

This notwithstanding, fortune favoured him at that time, and he handled himself so well in this charge with Demosthenes, that he took all the Spartans that they besieged, within the time he had appointed, saving such as were slain: and having made them yield, brought them prisoners to Athens. This fell out greatly to Nicias' shame and reproach.

But herein Nicias did great hurt to the commonwealth, suffering Cleon in that sort to grow to credit and estimation. For after that victory, Cleon grew to so haughty a mind and pride of himself, that he was not to be dealt withal: whereupon fell out the occasion of the great miseries that happened to the city of Athens, which most grieved Nicias of all other. For Cleon, amongst other things, took away the modesty and reverence used before in public orations to the people: he of all other was the first that cried out in his orations, that clapped his hand on his thigh, threw open his gown, and flung up and down the pulpit as he spake. Of which example afterwards followed all **licentiousness**, and contempt of honesty, the which all the orators and councillors fell into, that dealt in matters of state and commonwealth, and was in the end the overthrow of all together.

Part Two

In that very time began Alcibiades to grow to credit, by practise in the state, who was not altogether so corrupt, neither simply evil: but as they say of the land of Egypt, that for the **fatness and lustiness** of the soil,

> It bringeth forth both wholesome herbs, and also
> **noisome** weeds.

Even so Alcibiades' wit, excelling either in good or ill, was the cause and beginning of great change and alteration. For, it fell out, that after Nicias was rid of Cleon [*see next paragraph*], he could not yet bring the city of Athens again to peace and quietness. For when the commonwealth began to grow to some rest and reasonable good order, then was it again brought into wars, through Alcibiades' extreme fury of ambition. And thus it began.

The only peacebreakers and disturbers of common quiet generally throughout Greece, were these two persons, Cleon and Brasidas: for war cloaked the wickedness of the one, and advanced the valiantness of the other, giving to either [one] occasion to do great mischief, and also opportunity to work many noble exploits.

Now Cleon and Brasidas being both slain together at [the battle of Amphipolis], Nicias straight perceiving the Spartans had long desired peace, and that the Athenians were no more so hotly given to the wars, but that both the one and the other had their hands full, and were willing to be quiet: devised what means he might use to bring Sparta and Athens to reconciliation again, and to rid all the cities of Greece also from **broil** and misery of war, that thenceforth they might all together enjoy a peaceable and happy life. The rich men, the old men, and the **husbandmen**, he found very willing to **hearken** to peace: and talking privately also with divers others, he had so persuaded them, that he cooled them for being desirous of wars. Whereupon, putting the Spartans in good hope that all were inclined to peace, if they sought it: the Spartans believed him, not only for that they had found him at other times very soft and courteous, but also because he was careful to see that their prisoners of Sparta, (who had been taken at the fort of Pyle) were gently treated, and had made their miserable captivity more tolerable.

Narration and Discussion

What was the worst result (according to Plutarch) of Cleon's unexpected capture of the Spartans? What might have happened if Cleon had lost the battle?

How did Nicias bring the war to a temporary halt?

Lesson Four

Introduction

This lesson shows both the desire of (most) people to live in peace, and their fickleness when it comes to bestowing praise or blame.

Vocabulary

frequenting one another: building connections with each other

strangers: foreigners

amity: friendship

whose lot it was to begin: they agreed to decide by lot who should be the first to return prisoners or land

bought the lot: somehow arranged which side would get the "short straw"

privity: agreement

rendered up: surrendered

to set all things at stay: settle all issues

so far forth as: on the condition that

Ephors: the Lacedaemonian rulers

there fell out an earthquake: an earthquake interrupted the meeting

as he departed thence: in the same position as he had left

redelivered: released

captain: general

Historic Occasions

421 B.C.: the Peace of Nicias

Reading

Part One

So peace was concluded between the Spartans and the Athenians for a year, during which abstinence, they **frequenting one another** again, and beginning to taste the sweetness and pleasures of peace, and the safety of free access one to see another's friends that were **strangers**: began then to wish that they might still continue in peace and **amity** together, without effusion of blood of either party, and took great delight in their dances, to hear them sing such songs:

And let my spear lie overgrown, with dusty spiders' webs.

And so, upon a meeting together to talk of many matters, they made a universal peace throughout all Greece. Now most men thought that surely all their sorrows and miseries were come to an end, and there was no talk of any man but of Nicias, saying that he was a man beloved of the gods, who for his devotion towards them, had this special gift given him, that the greatest blessing that could come unto the world, was called after his name. For to confess a truth, every man was certainly persuaded that this peace was Nicias' work, as the war was Pericles' procurement, who upon light causes persuaded the Grecians to run headlong into most grievous calamities: and Nicias on the other side had brought them [all] to become friends, and to forget the great hurts the one had received of the other in former wars. And even to this present day, that peace is called *Nicium*, as who would say, Nicias' peace.

Part Two

The capitulations of the peace were thus agreed upon: that of either side they should alike deliver up the cities, and lands, which each had taken from other in time of wars, together with the prisoners also: and that they should first make restitution, **whose lot it was to begin**. Nicias (according to Theophrastus' report) for ready money secretly **bought the lot**, that the Lacedaemonians might be the first that should make restitution.

And when the Corinthians and Boeotians that disliked of this peace, sought by the complaints they made, to renew the war again: Nicias then persuaded both the Athenians and Lacedaemonians, that they should add for strength unto their country, the alliance and peace, offensive and defensive, made between them, for a more sure knot of frendship, whereby they might be the better assured the one of the other, and also the more dreadful to their enemies that should rebel against them. These things went clean against Alcibiades' mind: who besides that he was ill-born for peace, was enemy also unto the

Lacedaemonians, for that they sought to [please] Nicias, and made none account of him [Alcibiades], but despised him.

Here was the occasion that caused Alcibiades to prove from the beginning what he could do to hinder this peace, wherein he prevailed nothing. Yet shortly after, Alcibiades perceiving that the Athenians liked not so well of the Lacedaemonians as they did before, and that they thought themselves injured by them, because they had lately made league with the Boeotians without their **privity**, and had not wholly **rendered up** the cities of Panactum and Amphipolis according to the conditions articled between them: [he] began then to enlarge and aggravate the peoples' complaints, and to make them offended with every one of them. And furthermore he procured ambassadors from the city of Argos to come to Athens, and so handled the matter, that the Athenians made **league**, offensive and defensive, with them.

Part Three

While these matters were thus in hand, there came to Athens also ambassadors from Lacedaemon, with full power and authority **to set all things at stay**, and to compound all controversies: who having first spoken with the Senate, propounded things unto them both very honest and reasonable.

Whereupon, Alcibiades being afraid that they letting the people understand so much, should thereby bring them to yield to what they desired: he finely deceived the poor ambassadors by this device. He promised upon his oath to help them in that they went about, **so far forth as** they would not confess themselves to have absolute power from the **Ephors**: making them to believe it was the only way to bring their matters to pass.

The Ambassadors giving credit to his words, relied upon him, and so forsook Nicias. Whereupon Alcibiades brought them before the people being set in council, and there demanded openly of them, whether they had full power and authority to accord all matters yea or no. Whereunto they answer[ed] with a loud voice, that they had not *[as they had promised to say]*. Thereupon Alcibiades, contrary both to their expectation, and his own oath and promise made unto them: began to call the council to witness, whether they did not in open Senate say the contrary, and so advised the people not to trust nor give credit unto such men, as were openly taken with so manifest a lie, [who] would one while say one thing, another while another.

It boots not to ask whether the ambassadors were much amazed to hear Alcibiades' words: for Nicias himself wist not what to say to the matter, the suddenness of the cause did so confuse and grieve him, being a thing he least looked for. Now the people they were so moved besides, that they became indifferent whether to have sent for the ambassadors of Argos presently to have made league with them or not: but **there fell out an earthquake** upon this matter, that greatly served Nicias' turn, and brake up the assembly.

Part Four

The people meeting again in council the next morning, Nicias with all that he could do, or say, could scant withhold them from making league with the Argives *[those of Argos]*: and to get leave in the meantime to go to the Lacedaemonians, promising he would make all well again.

Thereupon, Nicias going to Sparta, was received and honoured there like a nobleman, and as one whom they thought well-affected towards them: but for the rest, he prevailed nothing, and being overcome by those that favoured the Boeotians, returned again to Athens **as he departed thence**. Where he was not only ill-welcomed home, and worse esteemed, but was also in danger of his person, through the fury of the people, that at his request and counsel had **redelivered** such men prisoners, and so great a number of them. For indeed, the prisoners which Cleon had brought to Athens from the fort of Pyle [Pylos], were all of the chiefest houses of Sparta, and their kinsmen and friends were the noblest men of the city. Notwithstanding, the people in the end did none other violence to him, saving that they chose Alcibiades their captain, and made league with the Elians, and Mantinians (which had revolted from the Lacedaemonians) and with the Argives also: and sent pirates to the fort of Pyle, to spoil the country of Laconia. Upon these occasions the Athenians fell again into wars.

Narration and Discussion

Why did Alcibiades want to stir up unrest? Was he successful?

Why was Nicias suddenly so unpopular when he returned to Athens?

Lesson Five

Introduction

It was officially time for an ostracism. Who would be voted out of Athens? Would it be "abominable" Alcibiades? Or would it be Nicias, who was disliked and envied in spite of his best efforts and his timorousness?

Vocabulary

his valiantness: Dryden translates this "his boldness and resolution," which still doesn't explain why they didn't value in Alcibiades what is usually seen as a good quality. (A good point for discussion!)

being no more familiar nor conversant with the people than he was: Nicias was not known for his friendliness

stately: haughty

haviour: behaviour, demeanour

discord and variance: disagreement

Sicily, Syracuse: Sicily is the very large island at the toe of Italy's "boot." Syracuse was a Greek colony (and city) in Sicily.

compassed chairs: chairs gathered together

against their inclination: against their better judgment

People

Egestans and Leontines: *Egesta* is the Greek word for Segesta, a city in Sicily. The Leontines were citizens of Leontini, also in Sicily.

Historic Occasions

415 B.C.: The Sicilian Expedition began

Reading

Part One

Now when the quarrel and controversy was greatest between Nicias and Alcibiades, the *Ostracismon* (to wit, the banishment for a time) came in, by the which the people banished for ten years any such of their citizens as they thought either of too great authority, or that was most envied for his wealth and substance.

Alcibiades and Nicias were then not a little perplexed, considering their present danger, being sure that the one of them two should not fail but be banished by this next banishment. For the people hated Alcibiades' life, and were **afraid of his valiantness**: as we have more amply declared in the description of his life. And for Nicias, his wealth made him to be envied; besides they misliked his strange manner of dealing, **being no more familiar nor conversant with the people than he was**, and counted him too **stately**: moreover they hated him also, because in many matters he had spoken directly against the thing the people desired, and had enforced them against their wills to agree to that which was profitable for themselves. In fine, to speak more plainly, there fell out great strife between the young men that would have wars, and the old men that coveted peace, some desirous to banish Nicias, and some others Alcibiades: but

> Where discord reigns in realm or town,

> The wicked win the chief renown.

And so fell it out then. For the Athenians being divided in two factions, gave authority to certain of the most impudent and insolent persons that were in all the city: and among them was one Hyperbolus, of the town of Perithus, a man of no **haviour** nor value, why he should be bold: but yet one that grew to some credit and power, dishonouring his country, by the honour they gave him. Now Hyperbolus thinking himself free at that time from any danger of banishment, (having rather deserved the gallows) hoping that if one of them two were banished, he should match [the one] well enough that remained behind: shewed openly, that he was glad of their **discord and variance**, and busily stirred up the people against them both.

Nicias and Alcibiades being acquainted with his wicked practices, having secretly talked together, joined both their factions in one: whereby they brought it so to pass, that neither of them were banished, but Hyperbolus [him]self for ten years. Which matter for the present time made the people very merry, though afterwards it grieved them much, seeing their ordinance of the *Ostracismon* blemished by the unworthiness of the person: which punishment was an honour unto him. For this banishment was thought a meet punishment for Thucydides, Aristides, and such like men of account as they, or their like: but for Hyperbolus, it was thought too great an honour, and too manifest an occasion of glory to be given to him, that for his wickedness had the selfsame punishment which was to be inflicted upon the chiefest estates for their greatness. And the comical poet Plato himself sayeth in a place:

> Although his lewd behavior did deserve as much or more,
>
> Yet was not that the punishment he should have had therefore.
>
> The Ostracy devised was for men of noble fame,
>
> And not for varlets, whose lewd life deserved open shame.

After this Hyperbolus, there was never man banished with the *Ostracismon*.

Part Two

Now the ambassadors of the **Egestans and Leontines** being come to Athens, to persuade the Athenians to attempt the conquest of **Sicily**: Nicias being against it, was overcome by Alcibiades' craft and ambition. For he, before they were called to council, had already through false surmises filled the people's heads with a vain hope and persuasion of conquest. Insomuch as the young men meeting in places of exercise, and the old men also in artificers' shops, and in their **compassed chairs**, or half circles where they sat talking together, were every one occupied about drawing the platform of

Sicily, telling the nature of the Sicilian sea, and reckoning up the havens and places looking towards Africa. For they made not their account that **Sicily** should be the end of their wars, but rather the storehouse and armoury for all their munition and martial provision to make war against the Carthaginians, and to conquer all Africa, and consequently all the African seas, even to Hercules' pillars.

Now all their minds being bent to wars, when Nicias spake against it, he found very few men of quality to stand by him. For the rich, fearing lest the people would think they did it to avoid [the public charges and ship-money, were quiet **against their inclination**; nevertheless he did not tire nor give it up.]

Narration and Discussion

Why were Nicias and Alcibiades willing to work together to get someone else ostracized? If you had a vote in the Ostracism, for whom would you have voted , and why?

Look at a map that shows Sicily. Why did the Athenians view it as a first step in conquering territory in Africa?

Lesson Six

Introduction

In the Sicilian Expedition, Nicias had the opportunity for a "defining moment." Pushed into a risky military venture, forced into a leadership role he didn't want, he nevertheless could choose to act heroically. Or he could scare everyone else into going home.

Vocabulary

holden: held

burdening: blaming

suborned: bribed, induced

prognosticate: foretell

descrying: looking carefully at

Egestans: see **Lesson Five**

the Athenians having sent for Alcibiades to answer to certain accusations: Alcibiades, from this point on, was no longer with the campaign

haven: harbour

discover: see what they could find out

Reading

Part One

But when they had passed the decree in council for the enterprise of Sicily, and [when] the people had chosen him chief captain, with Alcibiades and Lamachus to follow the same: at the next session of the council **holden** in the city, Nicias rose up again, to see if he could turn the people from this journey with all the protestations he could possibly make, **burdening** Alcibiades that, for his own ambition and private commodity, he brought the commonwealth into so far and dangerous a war.

But all his words prevailed not. [Nicias] before all others was thought the meetest man for this charge, partly because of his experience, but chiefly for [the fact] that they knew he would handle their matters with greater safety, when his timorous foresight should be joined with Alcibiades' valiantness, and with Lamachus' softness, which indeed most confirmed the election.

[Now after the matter thus debated, Demostratus, who, of the popular leaders, was the one who chiefly pressed the Athenians to the expedition, stood up and said he would stop the mouth of Nicias from urging any more excuses, and moved that the generals should have absolute power, both at home and abroad, to order and to act as they thought best; and this vote the people passed.]

Yet it is said that the priests objected many things to hinder the journey. But Alcibiades also having **suborned** certain soothsayers, alleged in like case some ancient oracles that said the Athenians should have great honour from Sicily: and further had enticed certain pilgrims, who said they were but newly come from the oracle of

Iupiter Ammon, and had brought this oracle thence, "That the Athenians should take all the Syracusans." But worst of all, if any knew of contrary signs or tokens to come, they held their peace, lest it should seem they intermeddled to **prognosticate** evil for affection's sake, seeing that the signs themselves, which were most plain and notorious, could not remove them from the enterprise of this journey. [*Omitted: certain religious statues in the city were vandalized at this time, and prophets warned against the invasion.*]

Part Two

Now for Nicias, that he spake against this war in open council, whilst they were deliberating upon it, and that he was not carried away with any vain hope, nor puffed up with the glory of so honourable a charge to make him change his mind: therein surely he shewed himself an honest man, wise, and constant. But when he saw plainly that he could by no persuasions remove the people from the enterprise of this war, neither yet by suit nor entreaty get himself discharged from being a captain thereof, but that they would in any case make him one of the heads of the army: then was it out of time to be fearful, and still giving back, turning his head so oft, like a child, to look upon his galley behind him, and ever to be telling that no reason could be heard in determining of this journey.

For indeed this was enough to discourage his companions, and to mar all at their first setting out: where, to say truly, he should suddenly have set upon his enemies, and have gone to it with a lusty courage, [and put fortune immediately to the test in battle]. But he took a clean contrary course. For Lamachus thought good, at their first coming, to go straight to Syracuse, and to give them battle as near the walls as might be; and Alcibiades, on the other side, was of opinion first of all to go about to win the cities that were in league with the Syracusans, and after that they had made them rebel, then to go against the Syracusans themselves. Nicias, to the contrary spake in council, and thought it better to go on fair and softly, **descrying** the coasts of Sicily round about to view their galleys and preparation, and so to return straight to Athens again, leaving only a few of their men with the **Egestans**, to help to defend them. But this from the beginning marvellously cooled the courage of the soldiers, and quite discouraged them.

Shortly after also, **the Athenians having sent for Alcibiades to answer to certain accusations**, Nicias remaining captain with Lamachus (the other captain [by title], but Nicias [him]self in power and authority, the lieutenant general of all the army) still used delays, running up and down, and spending time so long in consultation, till the soldiers were left without both hope and courage: and the fear the enemy had of them at their first coming to see so great an army, was now in manner clean gone.

Yet [with] Alcibiades (before he was sent for from Athens), they went with threescore galleys to Syracuse, of the which they placed fifty in battle [ar]ray out of the **haven**, and sent the other ten into the **haven** to **discover**: which approaching near the city, caused a herald to make open proclamation, that they were come thither to restore the **Leontines** to their lands and possessions.

Narration and Discussion

How was Nicias' "timorous foresight" again seen as an asset to Athens?

"He should suddenly have set upon his enemies, and have gone to it with a lusty courage...." Do you agree?

Lesson Seven

Introduction

The Sicilian Expedition continued, with what seemed mixed success. Nicias as a general was frustratingly slow to act, and let many opportunities slip. "Yet when he would do a thing indeed, he did it so thoroughly as no man could take exception to his doings, for that he brought it to so good a pass: and once taking it in hand, he did execute it with all speed..."

Vocabulary

pantofles: slippers

deferring of time still: delaying things

a pelting little town: Dryden translates this "a petty fortress"

Catana: a city on the eastern shore of Sicily, north of Syracuse

a baggage village: "a humble town"

they would come and enterprise the charge upon them first: the Syracusans had decided to attack the Athenians (instead of the other way round)

carriage: supplies

of this confederacy: in this conspiracy

without let or difficulty: without any interference

Hermocrates: the Syracusan general

which ran straight through Sicily: the news travelled quickly

Naxos: another city on the east coast of Sicily, about the same distance north of Catana as Catana was from Syracuse

for the doing of things of small moment...: they carried out a few minor raids

environed: surrounded

sick as he was of the stone: Nicias was ill with kidney stones

Reading

Part One

Now when Alcibiades was gone from the camp, Nicias bare all the sway and commanded the whole army. For Lamachus, though otherwise he was a stout man, an honest man, and very valiant of his hands, and one that would not spare himself in time of need: nevertheless he was so poor and miserable, that even when he was in state of a general, and gave up an account of his expenses, he would not stick to put into his books, so much for a gown, and so much for a pair of **pantofles**.

Nicias

Where Nicias' authority and reputation, contrarywise, was of another manner of cut, as well for other respects, as for his riches, and for the honour of many noble things which he had done before. As one [story] namely which they tell of him, that on a time being a captain with others, and sitting in council with his companions in the council house at Athens, about the dispatch of certain causes, he spake unto Sophocles the Poet, then present amongest them, and bade him speak first and say his opinion, being the oldest man of all the whole company. Sophocles answered him again: "Indeed I confess I am the oldest man, but thou art the noblest man, and him whom every man regardeth best."

So having at that time Lamachus under him, a better captain and man of war than himself was; yet by being so slow to employ the army under his charge **by deferring of time still**, and hovering about Siciy as far from his enemies as he could: he first gave the enemies time and leisure to be bold without fear of him. And then going to besiege Hybla, being but **a pelting little town**, and raising the siege without taking of it: he fell into so great a contempt with every man, that from thenceforth no man almost made any more reckoning of him.

At last, he retired unto **Catana** with his army, without any other exploit done, saving that he took Hyccara, **a baggage village** of the barbarous people.

And in fine, the summer being far spent, Nicias was informed that the Syracusans had taken such courage to them, that **they would come and enterprise the charge upon them first**: and that their horsemen were approached already before his camp, to skirmish with them, asking the Athenians in mockery, if they were come into Sicily to dwell with the Catanians, or to restore the Leontines to their lands again.

Hereupon with much ado, Nicias determined to go to Syracuse, and because he would camp there in safety, and at ease without hazard, he sent one of Catana before [them] to Syracuse, to tell them (as if he had been a spy) that if they would suddenly come and set upon the camp of the Athenians and take all their **carriage**, he wished them to come with all their power to Catana at a day certain which he would appoint them.

For the Athenians (said he) for the most part are within the city, wherein there are certain citizens, which, favouring the Syracusans, have determined so soon as they hear of their coming, to keep the gates of the city, and at the same time also to set the Athenians' ships afire: and how there were also a great number in the city **of this confederacy**, that did but look every hour for their coming.

And this was the noblest stratagem of war, that Nicias shewed all the time he was in Sicily. For by this device he made the Syracusans come into the field with all their power, so that they left their city without guard: and he himself departing in the meantime from Catana with all his fleet, won the haven of Syracuse at his ease, and chose out a place to camp in, where his enemies could not hurt him: in the which he was both the stronger, and might **without let or difficulty** set upon them with that, wherein he most trusted.

The Syracusans returning straight from Catana, and offering him battle hard by the walls of Syracuse, he came out into the field, and overthrew them. There were not many of the Syracusans slain at this battle, because their horsemen did hinder the chase: but Nicias, breaking up the bridges upon the river, gave **Hermocrates** occasion to mock him. For, comforting and encouraging the Syracusans, he told them Nicias deserved to be laughed at, because he did what he could that he might not fight, as if he had not purposely come from Athens to Syracuse to fight. This notwithstanding, he made the Syracusans quake for fear: for where they had then fifteen captains, they chose out three only, to whom the people were sworn, that they would suffer them to have full power and authority to command and take order for all things.

The temple of Iupiter Olympian was hard by the Athenians' camp, which they would gladly have taken, for that it was full of rich jewels and offerings of gold and silver, given unto the temple afore time. But Nicias of purpose still drave of time, and delayed so long, till the Syracusans at last sent a good garrison thither to keep it safe: thinking with himself, that if his soldiers came to take and spoil the temple, his country should be nothing the richer by it, and himself besides should bear all the blame of sacrilege.

Part Two

So, having obtained victory without profit, (**which ran straight through Sicily**) within few days after he returned unto the city of **Naxos**, where he lay all the winter, consuming a wonderful mass of victuals with so great an army, **for the doing of things of small moment, upon certain Sicilians that yielded to him.**

The Syracusans in the meantime being in heart again, and courageous: returned to **Catana**, where they spoiled and overran all the country, and burnt the camp of the Athenians. Herefore every man blamed Nicias much, because through his long delay, and protracting of time to make all things sure, he let slip sundry occasions of notable exploits, wherein good service might have been done. Yet when he would do a thing indeed, he did it so thoroughly as no man could take exception to his doings, for that he brought it to so good a pass: and once taking it in hand, he did execute it with all speed, though he was both slow to determine and a coward to enterprise.

Now when he removed his army to return to Syracuse, he brought it so orderly, and also with such speed and safety, that he was come by sea to Thapsus, had landed and taken the fort of Epipolis, before the Syracusans had any intelligence of it, or could possibly help it. For the choice men of the Syracusans being set out against him, hoping to have stopped his passage: he overthrew them, took three hundred prisoners and made their horsemen flee, which before were thought invincible. But that which made the Syracusans most afraid, and seemed most wonderful also to the other Grecians, was this: that in a very short space he had almost **environed** Syracuse with a wall, which was as much in compass about, as the walls of Athens, and worse to perform, by reason of the woody country, and for the sea also that beateth upon the walls. Besides that, there were divers marshes hard by it: and yet (**sick as he was of the stone**) he had almost finished it. And sure good reason it is that we attribute the fault of the not finishing of it, unto his sickness.

For mine own part I wonder marvellously both of the care and diligence of the captain, and of the valiantness and dexterity of the soldiers, which appeareth by the notable feats they did. For Euripides, after their overthrow and utter ruin, made a funeral epitaph in verse, and sayeth thus:

Eight times our men did put the men of Syracuse to flight,

So long as with indifferency the gods did use their might.

But we find it written, that the Syracusans were not only eight times, but many times more overthrown by them: a time at length there was indeed, that both the gods and fortune fought against them, even when the Athenians were of greatest power.

Discussion and Narration

Writing or interview assignment: In the format of a journal entry, letter, or oral interview, take the point of view of a member of the expedition to express your concerns. (You could also write from the Syracusan point of view.) Do you feel optimistic?

"...for where they had then fifteen captains, they chose out three only, to whom the people were sworn, that they would suffer them to have full power and authority to command and take order for all things." Why did this make the Syracusans "quake for fear?"

Plutarch said he admired Nicias "for what he succeeded in." Do you agree that his successes outweighed his disasters?

Lesson Eight

Introduction

We continue with the Athenians' attempt to take the city of Syracuse by building a wall around it. Alcibiades had left the expedition; Lamachus was also killed in the fighting, and that left Nicias, who made no secret of the fact that he didn't want to come in the first place, and who was suffering from kidney stones.

However, he put aside his reluctance and his physical problems, and led what could have been a successful siege; until some unexpected help arrived for the Syracusans.

Vocabulary

to keep: to ensure

abode him: engaged with him

they spurred cut for life: they ran

to set the wood afire...: they started a fire to keep the enemy away

that device only stayed the Syracusans: this was the one thing that saved the Athenians

fraught with corn: loaded with grain

parle: speak

a poor cape and wand of Lacedaemon: Dryden translates this "at the sight of one coarse coat and Laconian staff," or, just seeing a few tokens of Spartan power

by his procurement: by his persuasion

fell to his old trade: fell into his old way of thinking

People

Gylippus: the leader of a fleet sent by the Spartans to assist Syracuse

Reading

Part One

Now Nicias in his own person was ever in the greatest and most weighty affairs, striving with his sickly body. Howbeit one day when his disease grew sore upon him, he was compelled to be lodged in his camp with a few of his men: and Lamachus in the meantime alone having charge of the whole army, fought with the Syracusans, who then had brought a wall from the city, unto the wall with which the Athenians had purposed to have shut them in, **to keep** that they should not compass it round.

And because the Athenians commonly were the stronger in these skirmishes, they many times over-rashly followed the chase of their enemies that fled. As it chanced one day that Lamachus went so far, that he was left alone to encounter a company of horsemen of the city, before whom Callicrates marched foremost, a valiant man of his hands, who challenged Lamachus hand to hand. Lamachus **abode**

him, and in the conflict was first hurt: but he gave Callicrates also such a wound therewithal, that they both fell down dead presently in the place.

At that time the Syracusans being the stronger side, took up his body, and carried it away with them: but **they spurred cut for life** to the Athenians' camp, where Nicias lay sick, without any guard or succour at all: nevertheless, Nicias rose with speed out of his bed, and perceiving the danger he was in, commanded certain of his friends **to set the wood afire which they had brought within the trenches of the camp, to make certain devices for battery, and the engines of timber also that were already made. That device only stayed the Syracusans,** saved Nicias, and the strength of their camp, together with all the silver and carriage of the Athenians. For the Syracusans perceiving afar off, betwixt them and the strength of their camp, such a great flame as rose up in the air: upon sight of it turned tail straight, and made towards their city.

Things falling out thus, Nicias being left sole captain of the army without any companion, in great hope notwithstanding to do some good: divers cities of Sicily yielded unto him, ships **fraught with corn** came out of every quarter to his camp, and many submitted themselves, for the good success he had in all his doings. Furthermore the Syracusans also sent to **parle** with him of peace, being out of hope that they were able to defend their city any longer against him.

Gylippus also, a captain of the **Lacedaemonians,** coming to aid the Syracusans, understanding by the way how the city of Syracuse was shut in with a wall round about, and in great distress: held on his voyage notwithstanding, not with any hope to defend Sicily (supposing the Athenians had won the whole country) but with intent nevertheless to help the cities of Italy if he could possibly.

For it was a common rumour abroad, that the Athenians had won all, and that their captain for his wisdom and good fortune was invincible. Nicias himself now, contrary to his wonted wisdom and foresight, trusting altogether to the good success which he saw to follow him, but specially believing the reports that were told him of Syracuse, and the news that were brought him thence by some of themselves, which came secretly unto him, [believing they would almost immediately surrender the town upon terms]: took no care to withstand Gylippus' coming hither, neither sent any men to keep him from landing in Sicily. By which negligence, Gylippus landed in a passenger [ship], without Nicias' knowledge: so small reckoning they made of him, and so much did they fondly despise him.

Gylippus being thus landed far from Syracuse, began to gather men of war together, before the Syracusans themselves knew of his landing, or looked for his coming: insomuch as they had already appointed the assembly of a council to determine the articles and capitulations of peace, which they should conclude upon with Nicias.

Moreover, there were some that persuaded they should do well to make haste to conclude the peace, before the enclosure of Nicias' wall was altogether finished, which then lacked not much to perform, having all the stuff for the purpose brought even ready to the place.

Part Two

But as these things were even thus a-doing, arrived one Gongylus at Syracuse, that came from Corinth with a galley. At whose landing, the people upon the pier flocking about him, to hear what news: he told them that **Gylippus** would be there before it were long, and that there came certain other galleys after to their aid. The Syracusans would hardly believe him, untill there came another messenger also sent from Gylippus [him]self of purpose, that willed them to arm, and come to him into the field.

Thereupon the Syracusans being marvellously revived, went all straight and armed themselves. And Gylippus was no sooner come into Syracuse, but he presently put his men in battle [ar]ray, to set upon the Athenians. Nicias for his part had likewise also set the Athenians in order of battle, and ready to fight.

When both the armies were now approached near each to other, Gylippus threw down his weapons, and sent a herald unto Nicias to promise them life and baggage to depart safely out of Sicily. But Nicias would make the herald none answer to that message. Howbeit there were certain of his soldiers that in mockery asked the herald, if for the coming of **a poor cape and wand of Lacedaemon**, the Syracusans thought themselves strengthened so much, that they should despise the Athenians, which not long before kept three hundred Lacedaemonians [as] prisoners in irons, far stronger and [with] more hair on their heads than Gylippus had, and had also sent them home to their citizens at Lacedaemon.

And Timaeus writeth also, that the Sicilians themselves made no reckoning of Gylippus, neither then, nor at any time after. After, because they saw his extreme covetousness and misery: and then, for that he came so meanly apparelled, with a threadbare cape, and a long bush of hair, which made them scorn him. Yet in another place he sayeth, that so soon as Gylippus arrived in Sicily, many came to him out of every quarter with very good will, like birds wondering at an owl. This second report seemeth truer then the first: for they swarmed about him, because in this **"cape and wand"** they saw the tokens and the majesty of the city and **seigniory** of Sparta.

Thucydides also sayeth, that it was Gylippus only that did all there. And much like doth Philistus ([him]self a Syracusan) confess, who was present then in prison and saw all things that were done. Notwithstanding, at the first battle the Athenians had the upper hand, and slew a number of the Syracusans, among the which Gongylus the Corinthian was one.

But the morning following, Gylippus made them know the skill and experience of a wise captain. For, with the selfsame weapons, with the same men, with the same horses, and in the same places, changing only the order of his battle, he overthrew the Athenians: and (fighting with them still) having driven them even into their camp, he set the Syracusans to work to build up a wall overthwart, (with the very selfsame stones and stuff which the Athenians had brought and laid there for the finishing of their enclosure) to cut off the other, and to keep it from going forward, that it joined not together. So, all that the Athenians had done before until that present, was utterly to no purpose.

Things standing in these terms, the Syracusans, being courageous again, began to arm galleys, and running up and down the fields with their horsemen and slaves, took many prisoners. Gylippus, on the other side, went in person to and fro through the cities of Sicily, persuading and exhorting the inhabitants in such sort, that they all willingly obeyed him, and took arms **by his procurement**. Nicias, seeing things thus fall out, **fell to his old trade again**, and considering the change of his state and former good luck, his heart beginning to faint: wrote straight to the Athenians to send another army into Sicily, or rather to call that home which he had there, but in any case to give him leave to return, and to discharge him of his office, for cause of his sickness.

Discussion and Narration

Narrate the events around the arrival of Gylippus. Why was so little attention paid when his troops first landed?

Plutarch describes Gylippus as having "the skill and experience of a wise captain man of experience," and who could take "the selfsame weapons, the same men, the same horses," and fight successfully where another general failed. Have you seen a skilled person perform "miracles" with less-than-ideal equipment or circumstances?

Extra challenge

Write Nicias's letter to Athens, asking to be relieved of the command.

Lesson Nine

Introduction

Nicias pleaded for help against the Syracusans. The Athenians agreed to send reinforcements, with the promise that more help would arrive soon under Demosthenes. But the newly-arrived commanders seized their own chances for personal glory, and disaster followed.

Vocabulary

the store and tackle for many galleys: their naval supply

covered with: protected by

but for that: but only because

to prevent Demosthenes...: to jump the gun on him; do something great before he could get there

descried: spotted

hautboy: a musical instrument (oboe)

to fear: to frighten

straited a little more with want of victuals: put in a worse position by lack of food and supplies

People

Demosthenes, Eurymedon: Athenian generals sent to assist with the siege of Syracuse

Historic Occasions

414 B.C.: Athens sent ships to aid the expedition

Reading

Part One

The Athenians were indifferent before he wrote, to send aid thither: howbeit the envy the nobility bare unto Nicias' good fortune, did ever cause some delay [so] that they sent not, until then; and then they determined to send with speed. So **Demosthenes** was named to be sent away immediately after winter, with a great navy.

In the midst of winter, **Eurymedon** went to Nicias, and carried him both money and news, that the people had chosen some of them for his companions in the charge, which were already in service with him, to wit, Euthydemus and Menander. Now Nicias in the meantime being suddenly assailed by his enemies, both by sea and land: though at he first he had fewer galleys in number than they, yet he budged divers of theirs and sunk them. But by land again, he could not aid his men in time, because Gylippus at the first onset had taken a fort of his called Plemmyrion, within the which lay **the store and tackle for many galleys**, and a great mass of ready money which was wholly lost. Besides, in the same conflict also were many men slain, and many taken prisoners.

Yet further, the greatest matter of weight was, that thereby he took from Nicias the great commodity he had to bring his victuals safely by sea to his camp. For while the Athenians kept this fort, they might at their pleasure bring victuals without danger to their camp, being **covered with** the same: but when they had lost it, then it was hard for them so to do, because they were ever driven to fight with the enemies that lay at anchor before the fort. Furthermore, the Syracusans did not think that their army by sea was overthrown, because their enemies were the stronger, **but for that** their men had followed the Athenians disorderedly: and therefore were desirous once again to venture, in better sort and order than before.

But Nicias by no means would be brought to fight again, saying that it were a madness, looking for such a great navy and a new supply as **Demosthenes** was coming withal, rashly to fight with a fewer number of ships than they, and but poorly furnished. But contrarily, **Menander, and Euthydemus**, newly promoted to the state of captains with Nicias, being pricked forwards with ambition against the two other captains (**Nicias, and Demosthenes** that was then coming) desired **to prevent Demosthenes in performing some notable service before his arrival**, and thereby also to excel Nicias' doings. Howbeit, the cloak they had to cover their ambition withal was, the honour and reputation of the city of Athens, the which (said they) were shamed and dishonoured forever, if they now should shew themselves afraid of the Syracusans, who provoked them to fight.

Thus brought they Nicias against his will to battle, in the which the Athenians were slain and overcome, by the good counsel of a Corinthian pilot called **Ariston**. For the left wing of their battle (as Thucydides writeth) was clearly overthrown, and they lost a great number of their men.

Whereupon Nicias was wonderfully perplexed, considering on the one side that he had taken marvellous pains, whilst he was sole captain of the whole army: and on the other side, for that he had committed a foul fault, when they had given him companions.

But as Nicias was in this great despair, they **descried Demosthenes** upon a pier of the haven, with his fleet bravely set out and furnished, to terrify the enemies. For he had threescore and thirteen galleys, and in them he brought five thousand footmen well armed and appointed, and of darters, bowmen, and hurlers with slings about three thousand, and the galleys trimmed and set forth with goodly armours, numbers of ensigns, and with a world of trumpets, **hautboys**, and such marine music, and all set out in this triumphant show, **to fear** the enemies the more.

Part Two

Now thought the Syracusans themselves again in a peck of troubles, perceiving they strove against the stream, and consumed themselves to no purpose, when by that they saw there was no likelihood to be delivered from their troubles. And Nicias also rejoiced, that so great aid was come, but his joy held not long.

For so soon as he began to talk with Demosthenes of the state of things, he found him bent forthwith to set upon the Syracusans, and to hazard all with speed, that they might quickly take Syracuse, and so dispatch away home again. Nicias thought this more haste than good speed, and feared much this foolhardiness. Whereupon he prayed him to attempt nothing rashly, nor desperately: and persuaded him that it was their best way to prolong the war against the enemies, who were without money, and therefore would soon be forsaken of their confederates. And besides, if they came once to be pinched for lack of victuals: that they would then quickly seek to him for peace, as they had done aforetime. For there were many within Syracuse that were Nicias' friends, who wished him to abide time: for they were weary of war, and waxed angry also with Gylippus. So that if they were but **straited a little more with want of victuals**, they would yield straight [away]. Nicias, delivering these persuasions somewhat darkly, and keeping somewhat also from utterance, because he would not speak them openly: made his colleagues think he spake it for cowardliness, and that he returned again to his former delays to keep all in security, by which manner of proceeding he had from the beginning killed the hearts of his army, for that he had not at his first coming set upon the enemies, but had protracted time so long, till the courage of his soldiers was cold and done, and himself also brought into contempt with his enemies.

Whereupon the other captains (his colleagues and companions with him in the charge), **Euthydemus and Menander**, stuck to Demosthenes' opinion: whereunto Nicias was also forced against his will to yield.

Narration and Discussion

Imagine the conversation between Demosthenes and Nicias, as

Nicias pleaded with him to delay the battle in hopes that the Syracusans will give up.

Plutarch says that part of the problem was that Nicias did not speak plainly, but only made hints about the situation. Can you think of any Scriptures that describe the value of clear and honest speech?

Lesson Ten

Introduction

Under cover of night, the Athenians loaded their ships to return home, but they were frightened by an eclipse of the moon. "They concluded it to be ominous," Plutarch says, and it probably was; but what sabotaged their escape was fear, not fate.

Vocabulary

basing their pikes: raising their spears

apace: rapidly

targets: shields

appointed: equipped

betimes: early

motion: this is not a typo for "notion"; it can be read as "make a motion to do something"

natural philosophy: an early term for science

People

Anaxagoras: a Greek philosopher (510-428 B.C.) who explained eclipses

Reading

Part One

So Demosthenes the selfsame night taking the footmen, went to assault the fort of Epipolis: where, before his enemies heard anything of his coming, he slew many of them, and made the rest flee that offered resistance.

But not content with this victory, he went further, till he fell upon the Boeotians. They, gathering themselves together, were the first that resisted the Athenians, **basing their pikes** with such fury and loud cries, that they caused the [Athenians] to retire, and made all the rest of the assailants afraid and amazed. For the foremost [of them] fleeing back, came full upon their companions: who, taking them for their enemies, and their flight for a charge, resisted them with all their force, and so mistaking one another, both were wounded and slain, and the hurt they meant unto their enemies, did unfortunately light upon their own fellows.

For this multitude meeting thus confusedly together, what through their great fear, and what for that they could not discern one another in the night, the which was neither so dark that they could not see at all, nor yet so clear, as they might certainly judge by sight what they were that met them. (For then the moon declined **apace**, and the small light it gave was diffused with the number of men that ran to and fro.) The fear they had of the enemy made them mistrust their friends.

All these troubles and disadvantages had the Athenians, and beside, the moon on their backs, which, causing the shadow to fall forward, did hide their number; and contrarily, the enemies' **targets**, glaring in their eyes by the reflection of the moon that shone upon them, increased their fear, and making them seem a greater number and better **appointed** than they were indeed. At last, the enemies giving a lusty charge upon them on every side, after they once began to give back and turn tail: some were slain by their enemies, others by their own company, and others also brake their necks falling from the rocks. The rest that were dispersed abroad in the fields, were the next morning every man of them put to the sword by the horsemen. So, the account made, two thousand Athenians were slain, and very few of them escaped by flight, that brought their armours back again.

Wherefore Nicias, that always mistrusted it would thus come to pass, was marvellously offended with Demosthenes, and condemned his rashness. But he [Demosthenes], excusing himself as well as he could, thought it best to embark in the morning **betimes**, and so to hoist sail homewards. For, said he, we must look for no new aid from Athens, neither are we strong enough with this army to overcome our enemies: and though we were, yet must we of necessity avoid the place we are in, because (as it is reported) it is always unwholesome for an army to camp in, and then specially most contagious, by reason of the autumn and season of the year, as they might plainly see by experience. For many of their people were already sick, and all of them in manner had no mind to tarry.

Nicias in no case liked the **motion** of departing thence, because he feared not the Syracusans, but rather the Athenians, for their accusations and condemnation. And therefore in open council he told them, that as yet he saw no such danger to remain: and though there were, yet that he had rather die of his enemies' hands, than to be put to death by his own countrymen. And furthermore, as for removing their camp to some other place, they should have leisure enough to determine of that matter as they thought good.

Now when Nicias had delivered this opinion in council, Demosthenes having had ill luck at his first coming, durst not contrary it. And the residue also supposing that Nicias stuck not so hard against their departure, but that he relied upon the trust and confidence he had of some within the city: they all agreed to Nicias. But when news came that there was a new supply come unto the Syracusans, and that they saw the plague increased more and more in their camp: then Nicias [him]self thought it best to depart thence, and gave notice to the soldiers to prepare themselves to ship away.

Part Two

Notwithstanding, when they had put all things in readiness for their departure, without any knowledge of the enemy, or suspicion thereof: the moon began to eclipse in the night, and suddenly to lose her light, to the great fear of Nicias and divers others, who through ignorance and superstition quaked at such sights. For, touching the eclipse and darkening of the sun, which is ever at any conjunction of the moon, every common person then knew the cause to be the darkness of the body of the moon betwixt the sun and our sight. But the eclipse of the moon itself, to know what doth darken it in that sort, and how being at the full it doth suddenly lose her light, and change into so many kind of colours: that was above their knowledge, and therefore they thought it very strange, persuading themselves that it was a sign of some great mischiefs the gods did threaten unto men.

For **Anaxagoras**, the first that ever determined and delivered anything, for certain and assured, concerning the light and darkness of the moon: his doctrine was not then of any long continuance, neither had it the credit of antiquity, nor was generally known, but only to a few, who durst not talk of it but with fear even to them they trusted best. And the reason was, for that the people could not at that time abide them that professed the knowledge of **natural philosophy**, and inquired of the causes of things: for them they called [theorists], as much to say, as curious inquirers, and tattlers of things above the reach of reason, done in heaven and in the air. Because the people thought they ascribed that which was done by the gods only, unto certain natural and necessary causes, that work their effects not by providence nor will, but by force, and necessary consequences.

But then it fell out unfortunately for Nicias, who had no expert nor skillful soothsayer: for the party which he was wont to use for that purpose, and which took away much of his superstition, called Stilbides, was dead not long before. For this sign of the eclipse of the moon (as Philochorus [observes]) was not hurtful for men that would flee, but contrarily very good: for said he, things that men do in fear, would be hidden, and therefore light is an enemy unto them. [Nor was it usual to observe signs in the sun or moon more than three days, as Autoclides states in his Commentaries. But Nicias persuaded them to wait another full course of the moon, as if he had not seen it clear again as soon as ever it had passed the region of shadow where the light was obstructed by the earth.]

Narration and Discussion

Why was Nicias more afraid of the Athenians than he was of the Syracusans?

Plutarch says that an eclipse of the moon would actually be a very good "omen" for the Athenians, because the darkness would help them escape. How did Nicias fail to make the most of this opportunity?

Why did people feel it would lessen the power of the gods if they looked for scientific reasons for things that happened? Were they right? Should the same viewpoint limit the interest of Christians in science?

Lesson Eleven

Introduction

Could the Athenians could somehow get away from Syracuse without all being killed or taken captive? Nicias believed it was possible.

This is a complex lesson, so it may be better to read it in more than one sitting.

Vocabulary

haven: harbour

light barks: small boats

shamefully reviled them: taunted them

amain: quickly

retire: retreat

wonted: usual

mortal: fatal

alteration: turn(s) of fortune

which were to end their lives with much more cruelty: they
    expected to be taken as prisoners and treated cruelly or killed

by peep of day: at daybreak

People

Gylippus: the Spartan general sent to aid Syracuse (see **Lesson Eight**)

Hermocrates: the Syracusan general (see **Lesson Seven**)

Historic Occasions

413 B.C.: The Second Battle of Syracuse

Reading

Part One

But all other things laid aside and forgotten, Nicias disposed himself
to sacrifice unto the gods: until such time as the enemies came again
as well to besiege their forts, and all their camp by land, as also to
occupy the whole **haven** by sea. For they [the enemy] had not only
put men aboard into their galleys able to wear armour, but moreover
young boys into fisher boats and other **light barks**, with the which
they came to the Athenians, and **shamefully reviled them**, to
procure them to fight: among the which there was one of a noble
house, called Heraclides, whose boat being forwarder than his
companions, was in danger of [being taken] by a galley of the
Athenians, that rowed against him. Pollichus, his uncle, being afraid
of it, launched forward with ten galleys of Syracuse for his rescue, of
the which himself was captain. The other galleys doubting also lest
Pollichus should take hurt, came on likewise **amain**: so that there fell
out a great battle by sea, which the Syracusans won, and slew
Eurymedon, the [Athenian] captain, and many other[s].

This made the soldiers of the Athenians so afraid, that they began
to cry out [that] it was no longer [any use] tarrying there, and that
there was none other way but to depart thence by land. For after the
Syracusans had won that battle, they had straight shut up the **haven**
mouth.

Nicias could not consent to such a **retire**. For, said he, it would be
too great a shame for them to leave their galleys and other ships to
the enemy, considering the number not to be much less then two
hundred: but he thought good rather to arm **a hundred and ten**

galleys with the best and valiantest of their footmen and darters, because the other galleys had spent their oars. And for the rest of the army, Nicias, forsaking their great camp and walls (which reached as far as the temple of Hercules) did set them in battle [ar]ray upon the pier of the **haven**. Insomuch, that the Syracusans, which until that day could not perform their **wonted** sacrifices unto Hercules, did then send their priests and captains thither to do them.

The soldiers being embarked into the galleys, the priests and soothsayers came and told the Syracusans that undoubtedly the signs of the sacrifices did promise them a noble victory, so that they gave no charge, but only stood upon their defense: for so did Hercules ever overcome, defending, when he was assailed.

Part Two

With this good hope the Syracusans rowed forward, and there was such a hot and cruel battle by sea, as had not been in all this war before: the which was as dreadful to them that stood on the shore to behold it, as it was **mortal** unto them that fought it, seeing the whole conflict, and what **alteration** fell out beyond all expectation. For the Athenians did as much hurt themselves by the order they kept in their fight, and by the ranks of their ships, as they were hurt by their enemies. For they had placed all their great ships together, fighting with the heavy [ones], against the enemies' [ships] that were light and swift, which came on on every side of them, whirling stones at them which were made sharp to wound however they lighted: whereas the Athenians only casting their darts, and using their bows and slings, by means of their rowing up and down could not lightly aim to hit with the head. That manner of fight, Aristo a Corinthian (an excellent shipmaster) had taught the Syracusans, who was himself slain valiantly fighting, when they were conquerers.

The Athenians thereupon being driven to fight, having sustained marvellous slaughter and overthrow, (their way to flee by sea being also clearly taken from them) and perceiving moreover that they could hardly save themselves by land, were then so discouraged as they made no longer resistance when their enemies came hard by them and carried away their ships before their faces. Neither did they ask leave to take up their dead men's bodies to bury them, taking more pity to forsake their diseased and sore wounded companions, than to bury them that were already slain. When they considered all these things, they thought their own state more miserable than theirs, **which were to end their lives with much more cruelty**, than was their misery [at] present.

Part Three

So [as the Athenians had] determined to depart thence in the night, **Gylippus**, perceiving the Syracusans through all the city disposed themselves to sacrifice to the gods, and to be merry, as well for the joy of their victory, as also for Hercules' feast; [he] thought it bootless to persuade them, and much less to compel them, to take arms upon a sudden, to set upon their enemies that were departing.

Howbeit **Hermocrates**, devising with himself how to deceive Nicias, sent some of his friends unto him with instructions, to tell him that they came from such as were wont to send him secret intelligence of all things during this war: and willed him to take heed not to depart that night, lest he fall into the ambushes which the Syracusans had laid for him, having sent before to take all the straits and passages, by the which he should pass. Nicias being overreached by Hermocrates' craft and subtlety, stayed there that night, as though he had been afraid to fall within the danger of his enemies' ambush.

Thereupon, the Syracusans the next morning by peep of day, hoist[ed] sail, got the straits of Nicias' passage, stopped the rivers' mouths, and brake up the bridges: and then cast their horsemen in a squadron in the next plain fields adjoining, so that the Athenians had no way left to escape, and pass by them, without fighting.

At last, notwithstanding, having stayed all that day and the next night following, they put themselves in journey, and departed with great cries and lamentations, as if they had gone from their natural country, and not out of their enemies' land: as well for the great distress and necessity wherein they were, (lacking all things needful to sustain life) as also for the extreme sorrow they felt to leave their sore wounded companions and diseased kinsmen and friends behind them, that could not for their weakness follow the camp, but specially for that they looked for some worse matter to fall to themselves, than that which they saw present before their eyes [which had] happened to their fellows.

But of all the most pitiful sights to behold in that camp, there was none more lamentable nor miserable, than the person of Nicias [him]self: who being tormented with his disease, and waxen very lean and pale, was also unworthily brought to extreme want of natural sustenance, even when he had most need of comfort, being very sickly. Yet notwithstanding his weakness and infirmity, he took great pains, and suffered many things, which the soundest bodies do labour much to overcome and suffer: making it appear evidently to every man, that he did not abide all that pains for any respect of himself, or desire that he had to save his own life, so much as for their sakes in that he yielded not unto present despair. For where the soldiers for very fear and sorrow burst out into tears and bitter wailing: Nicias [him]self shewed, that if by chance he were forced at any time to do the like, it was rather upon remembrance of the shame and dishonour that came into his mind, to see the unfortunate success of this voyage, instead of the honour and victory they hoped to have brought home, than for any other respect.

But if to see Nicias in this misery did move the lookers-on to pity, yet did this much more increase their compassion, when they remembered Nicias' words in his orations continually to the people, to break this journey, and to dissuade them from the enterprise of this war. For then they plainly judged him not to have deserved these troubles. Yet furthermore, this caused the soldiers utterly to despair of help from the gods, when they considered with themselves, that so devout and godly a man as Nicias (who left nothing undone that might tend to the honour and service of the gods) had no better success than the most vile and wicked persons in all the whole army.

Narration and Discussion

Describe the battle in the harbour. What advantages did the Syracusans have?

How did Hermocrates deceive Nicias?

In Dryden's words, the soldiers had no "heart to put their trust in the gods, considering that a man so religious, who had performed to the divine powers so many and so great acts of devotion, should have no more favourable treatment than the wickedest and meanest of the army." Were they right? If you could travel back in time, would you agree with them about the futility of continuing to sacrifice to the gods? Consider how you would respond if they asked if your God would also allow his faithful ones to suffer.

Lesson Twelve

Introduction

In this, the last passage on the life of Nicias, we hear little more of him other than the manner of his death. "The fortunes of war are common," he pleaded with Gylippus, with a thought that echoes the end of *Pyrrhus*.

Plutarch's attention at the end shifts to the fates of the other Athenians and their slaves. But in the midst of this chaos, some of them find themselves saved by...poetry.

Vocabulary

bands: troops

understand: discover

hearken to: consider

victuals: food, supplies

residue: remaining

divers: some of them

government: leadership

cusinges: Dryden translates this "tiles"

bewrayed: betrayed

the haven of Piraea: the harbour used by Athens

People

Demosthenes: one of the Athenian commanders (see Lesson **Nine**)

Gylippus: the Spartan general sent to aid Syracuse (see **Lesson Eight**)

Hermocrates: the Syracusan general (see **Lesson Seven**)

Euripides: an Athenian playwright (480-406 B.C.)

Reading

Part One

All this notwithstanding, Nicias strained himself in all that might be, both by his good countenance, his cheerful words, and his kind using of every man: to let them know that he fainted not under his burden, nor yet did yield to this his misfortune and extreme calamity. And thus travelling eight days' journey outright together, notwithstanding that he was by the way continually set upon, wearied, and hurt: yet he ever maintained his **bands**, and led them whole in company until that **Demosthenes**, with all his **bands** of soldiers, was taken prisoner, in a certain village called Polyzelios: where remaining behind, he was environed by his enemies in fight, and seeing himself so compassed in, drew out his sword, and with his own hands thrust himself through, but died not of it, because his enemies came straight about him, and took hold of him.

The Syracusans thereupon went with speed to Nicias, and told him of Demosthenes' case. He, giving no credit to them, sent presently certain of his horsemen thither to **understand** the truth: who brought him word that Demosthenes and all his men were taken prisoners. Then he besought **Gylippus** [for a truce for the Athenians to depart out of Sicily, leaving hostages for payment of money that the Syracusans had expended in the war].

Howbeit the Syracusans would in no wise **hearken to** peace, but cruelly threatening and reviling them that made motion hereof, in rage gave a new onset upon him, more fiercely than ever before they had done. Nicias being then utterly without any kind of **victuals**, did notwithstanding hold out that night, and marched all the next day following (though the enemies' darts still flew about their ears) until he came to the river of Asinarus, into the which the Syracusans did forcibly drive them.

Some others of them also dying for thirst, entered the river of themselves, thinking to drink. But there of all others was the most cruel slaughter of the poor wretches, even as they were drinking: until such time as Nicias falling down flat at Gylippus' feet, said thus unto him: "Since the gods have given thee (Gylippus) victory, shew mercy, not to me that by these miseries have won immortal honour and fame, but unto these poor vanquished Athenians: calling to thy remembrance, that the fortunes of war are common, and how that the Athenians have used you Lacedaemonians courteously, as often as fortune favoured them against you."

Gylippus beholding Nicias, and persuaded by his words, took compassion of him (for he knew he was a friend unto the Lacedaemonians at the last peace concluded betwixt them, and furthermore thought it great honour to him, if he could carry away the two captains or generals of his enemies [as] prisoners); shewed him mercy, gave him words of comfort, and moreover commanded besides that they should take all the **residue** prisoners. But his commandment was not known in time to all: insomuch as there were many more slain than taken, although some private soldiers saved **divers** notwithstanding by stealth.

Now the Syracusans having brought all the prisoners that were openly taken into a troop together, first unarmed them, then taking their weapons from them hung them up upon the goodliest young trees that stood upon the river's side in token of triumph And so putting on triumphing garlands upon their heads, and having trimmed their own horses in triumphant manner, and also shorn all the horses of their enemies, in this triumphing sort they made their entry into the city of Syracuse, having gloriously ended the most notable war that ever was amongst the Greeks one against another, and attained also the noblest victory that could be achieved, and that only by force of arms and valiancy.

Part Two

[And a general assembly of the people of Syracuse and their confederates sitting, Eurycles, the popular leader, moved, first, that the day on which they took Nicias should from thenceforward be kept holiday by sacrificing and forbearing all manner of work, and from the river he called the Asinarian Feast. This was the twenty-sixth day of the month Carneus, the Athenian Metagitnion. And that the servants of the Athenians with the other confederates be sold for slaves, and they themselves and the Sicilian auxiliaries be kept and employed in the quarries, except the generals, who should be put to death.] And when the captain **Hermocrates** went about to persuade them that to be merciful in victory woul be more honour unto them than the victory itself, they thrust him back with great tumult.

And furthermore, when Gylippus made suit that for the captains of the Athenians, he might carry them alive with him to Sparta: he was not only shamefully denied, but most vilely abused, so lusty were they grown upon this victory, beside also that in the time of the war they were offended with him, and could not endure his severe Laconian **government**. Timaeus sayeth moreover, that they accused him (Gylippus) of covetousness and theft, which vice he inherited from his father. For Cleandrides his father was convict[ed] for extortion, and banished [from] Athens. And Gylippus [him]self having stolen thirty talents out of a thousand which Lysander sent to Sparta by him, and having hid them under the **cusinges** of his house, being **bewrayed**, was compelled with shame to flee his country, as we have more amply declared in the *Life of Lysander*.

Part Three

So Timaeus writeth, that Nicias and Demosthenes were not stoned to death by the Syracusans, as Thucydides and Philistus report, but that they killed themselves, upon word sent them by Hermocrates (before the assembly of the people was broken up) by one of his men whom the keepers of the prison let in unto them: howbeit their bodies were cast out at the jail door for every man to behold.

As for the other prisoners of the Athenians, the most of them died of sickness, and of ill handling in the prison: where they had no more allowed them to live withal but two dishfuls of barley for their bread, and one of water for each man a day. Indeed many of them were conveyed away, and sold for slaves: and many also that [e]scaped unknown as slaves, were also sold for bondmen, whom they branded in the forehead with the print of a horse, who notwithstanding besides their bondage endured also this pain. But such, their humble patience and modesty did greatly profit them. For either shortly after they were made free men, or if they still continued in bondage, they were gently treated, and beloved of their masters.

Some of them were saved also for **Euripides'** sake. For the Sicilians liked the verses of this poet better than they did any other Grecian's verses. For if they heard any rhymes or songs like unto his, they would have them by heart, and one would present them to another with great joy. And therefore it is reported, that **divers** escaping this bondage, and returning again to Athens, went very lovingly to salute Euripides, and to thank him for their lives: and told him how they were delivered from slavery, only by teaching them those verses which they remembered of his works. Others told him also, how that after the battle, they [e]scaping by flight, and wandering up and down the fields, met with some that gave them meat and drink to sing his verses. And this is not to be marvelled at, weighing the report made of a ship of the city of Caunus, that on a time being chased in thither by pirates, thinking to save themselves within their ports, could not at the first be received, but had repulse: howbeit being demanded whether they could sing any of Euripides' songs, and answering that they could, were straight suffered to enter, and come in.

Part Four

The news of this lamentable overthrow was not believed, at the first, when they heard of it at Athens. For a stranger that landed in **the haven of Piraea**, went and sat him down (as the manner is) in a barber's shop, and thinking it had been commonly known there, began to talk of it. The barber, hearing the stranger tell of such matter before any other had heard of it, ran into the city as fast as he could, and going to the governors told the news openly before them all.

The magistrates thereupon did presently call an assembly, and brought the barber before them: who being demanded of whom he heard these news, could make no certain report. At last there arrived certain men in the city, who brought certain news thereof, and told how the overthrow came. So as in fine they found Nicias' words true, which now they believed, when they saw all those miseries light fully upon them, which he long before had prognosticated unto them.

Narration and Discussion

Explain Nicias's words to Gylippus: "Since the gods have given thee (Gylippus) victory, shew mercy, not to me that by these miseries have won immortal honour and fame, but unto these poor vanquished Athenians: calling to thy remembrance, that the fortunes of war are common, and how that the Athenians have used you Lacedaemonians courteously, as often as fortune favoured them against you." Why did Gylippus respond as he did?

Ray Bradbury's book *Fahrenheit 451* takes place in a time when books are outlawed. The main character discovers a secret community of people who have each memorized one piece of literature...a sort of living library. Similarly, some of the Athenians escaped death or slavery by being able to repeat something they had memorized. What do you think would be most valuable to know by heart?

Plutarch says that the Syracusans "gloriously ended the most notable war that ever was amongst the Greeks one against another." Why was this battle so important in history?

The Plutarch Project

Crassus
(ca. 115 B.C. – 53 B.C.)

Introduction

You are about to meet a wealthy and powerful ruler from the last days of the Roman Republic; someone who crushed a world-famous slave rebellion; and someone who, as the Roman governor of Syria, led his army to one of the worst defeats in Roman history. Yet until now you may not have ever heard his name.

By the end of the study, you will be among those who do remember the name of Crassus. You may admire him or not; you may like him, or you may not; but you won't forget him.

Who was Crassus?

Marcus Licinius Crassus, also called Marcus Licinius Crassus Dives, was a general, a politician, and one of the richest men in history (*Dives* means "wealthy"). He was one of the First Triumvirate, a group of three leaders that also included Julius Caesar and Pompey.

Lesson One

Introduction

In board games, one player often grows rich by acquiring properties: sometimes from the "bank," but also from others who find themselves in trouble. The Roman leader Crassus began life in a less-than-magnificent style; but he was determined to change that.

Vocabulary

censor: one of the highest public offices in Rome

the honour of triumph: public recognition of success in a battle

corn: grain

when he went from Rome to make war with the Parthians: Crassus, late in his life, led an army against the Parthians (the best archers in the world.) See **Lesson Seven.**

portsale: public auction

bondmen: indentured servants; slaves

hinds: farm assistants

scriveners: scribes, secretaries

husband: steward, manager

usury: unfair financial advantage

painful: painstaking

were he never so mean: no matter how low in position the man was

a hat to cover his head: Dryden translates this "cloak."

did not place poverty in things indifferent: even the philosophy of Aristotle did not teach that poverty was of no matter

People

Sulla: A Roman general, the rival of Marius (see below). The seizing of Rome referred to here took place in 82 B.C., when Crassus was about 33 years old. When Sulla took power, he needed a way to pay back those in his army who had helped him gain the victory; so he began a kind of "reign of terror" in which many supposedly disloyal aristocrats were executed and their valuable properties were seized.

Marius: A general and ruler of Rome who was responsible for the deaths of Crassus' father and brother.

Alexander: A close companion of Crassus, possibly a longtime member of the household who may have had a hand in Crassus' education.

Reading

Marcus Crassus was the son of a censor, who had also received the honour of triumph: but himself was brought up in a little house with two other[s] of his brethren, which were both married in their father's and mother's lifetime, and kept house together. Whereupon it came to pass, that he was a man of such sober and temperate diet, that one of his brethren being deceased, he married his [brother's] wife, by whom he had children.

The Romans say there was but that only vice of covetousness in Crassus, that drowned many other goodly virtues in him: for mine own opinion, methinks he could not be touched with that vice alone without others, since it grew so great, as the note of that only did hide and cover all his other vices. Now to set out his extreme covetous desire of getting, naturally bred in him, they prove it by two manifest reasons. The first, his manner and means he used to get: and the second, the greatness of his wealth. For at the beginning he was not left much more worth, then three hundred talents. And during the time that he dealt in the affairs of the commonwealth, he offered the tenths of all his goods wholly unto Hercules, kept open house for all the people of Rome, and gave also to every citizen of the same as much **corn** as would keep him three months: and yet **when he went from Rome to make war with the Parthians**, himself being desirous to know what all he had was worth, found that it amounted to the sum of seven thousand one hundred talents. But if I may with license use evil speech, writing a truth: I say he got the most part of his wealth by fire and blood, raising his greatest revenue of public calamities. For when Sulla had taken the city of Rome, he (Sulla) made **portsale** of the goods of them whom he had put to death, to those that gave most, terming them his booty, only for that he would the nobility, and greatest men of power in the city should be partakers with him of this iniquity: and in this open sale Crassus never left [off] taking of gifts, nor buying of things of Sulla for profit.

Furthermore, Crassus perceiving that the greatest decay commonly of the buildings in Rome came by fire, and falling down of houses, through the overmuch weight by numbers of storeys built one upon another: [he] bought **bondmen** that were masons, carpenters, and these devisers and builders, and of those he had to the number of five hundred. Afterwards, when the fire took any house, he would buy the house while it was a-burning, and the next houses adjoining to it, which the owners sold for little, being then in danger as they were, and a-burning: so that by process of time, the most part of the houses in Rome came to be his. But notwithstanding that he had so many slaves to his workmen, he never built any house from the ground, saving his own house wherein he dwelt: saying, that such as delighted to build, undid themselves without help of any enemy. And though he had many mines of silver, many ploughs, and a number of **hinds** and plowmen to follow the same: yet all that commodity was nothing, in respect of the profit his slaves and bondmen brought him daily in. As readers, **scriveners**, goldsmiths, bankers, receivers, stewards of household, carvers, and other such officers at the table, taking pains himself to help them when they were learners, and to instruct them what they should do: and to be short, he thought the greatest care a good householder ought to have, was to see his slaves or servants well taught, being the most lively cattle and best instruments of a man's house. And surely therein his opinion was not ill, at the least if he thought as he spake: that all things must be done by servants, and his servants must be ruled by him. For we see that the art and skill to be a good **husband**, when it consisteth in government of things without life or sense, is but a base thing, only tending to gain: but when it dependeth upon good order and government of men, methinks then it is to know how to govern well a commonwealth. But as his judgement was good in the other, so was it very bad in this: that he thought no man rich, and wealthy, that could not maintain a whole army with his own proper goods. For the war (as King Archidamus was wont to say) is not made with any certainty of expense: and therefore there must no sufficiency of riches be limited for the maintenance of the same. But herein Marius and he differed far in opinion: who having allowed every Roman fourteen acres [of] land (called with them *ingera*) understanding that some were not pleased, but would have more, made them this answer: The gods forbid any Roman should think that land little, which indeed is enough to suffice for his maintenance.

This notwithstanding, Crassus was courteous to strangers, for his house was open to them all, and he lent his friends money without interest: but when they brake day of payment with him, then would he roundly demand his money of them. So, his courtesy to lend many times without interest, did more trouble them, than if he had taken very great **usury**. Indeed when he bade any man to come to his table, his fare was but even ordinary, without all excess: but his fine and cleanly service, and the good entertainment he gave every man that came to him, pleased them better, than if he had been more plentiful of diet and dishes.

As for his learning and study, he chiefly studied eloquence, and that sort specially that best would serve his turn to speak in open presence: so that he became the best spoken man in Rome of all his time, and by his great industry and diligent endeavor excelled all them that even by nature were most apt unto it. For some say, he had never so small nor little a cause in hand, but he always came prepared, having studied his case before for pleading: and oftentimes also when Pompey, Caesar, and Cicero refused to rise, and speak to matters, Crassus would defend every cause if he were requested. And therefore was he generally beloved and well thought of, because he shewed himself **painful**, and willing to help every man. Likewise was his gentleness marvellously esteemed, because he saluted everybody courteously, and made much of all men: for, whomsoever he met in the streets that spake to him as he passed and saluted him, **were he never so mean**, he would speak to him again, and call him by his name.

It is said also he was very well studied in stories, and indifferently seen in philosophy, specially in Aristotle's works, which one **Alexander** did read unto him, a man that became very gentle and patient of nature, by using of Crassus' company: for it were hard to say, whether Alexander was poorer when he came to Crassus or made poorer while he was with him. Of all his friends he would ever have Alexander abroad with him, and while they were abroad, would lend him **a hat to cover his head** by the way: but so soon as they were returned, he would call for it again. O wonderful patience of a man! To see that he making profession of philosophy as he did, the poor man being in great poverty, **did not place poverty in things indifferent**. But hereof we will speak more hereafter.

Narration and Discussion

In the *Life of Nicias*, Plutarch said that his purpose in writing was "to decipher the man and his nature." How does he attempt to prove Crassus' vice of covetousness? What other characteristics do you notice?

Does the story about the mistreatment of Alexander show only how miserly Crassus could be? Or was Alexander trying to make a point about earthly wealth by his longsuffering?

Lesson Two

Introduction

Part One begins with a flashback to 87 B.C., about five years before the time of **Lesson One**, when Crassus was almost thirty years old. In that year, Marius was elected to his seventh consulship, along with Cinna, and they killed off many enemies, including the father and brother of Crassus. Plutarch says that because Crassus was young, he wasn't high on the list, but that he was still in some danger; so he escaped to Spain until he heard that Cinna was dead. (As a note of interest, Cinna was Julius Caesar's father-in-law.)

Crassus raised an army and arrived back in Rome in time to help Sulla fight a very bloody civil war against the Marians (supporters of Marius), and in 82 B.C. Sulla declared himself dictator (sole ruler). He then carried out his own "reign of terror," when those who had opposed him (or were merely suspected to have opposed him) were put to death. Crassus supported and helped with the war and its terrible aftermath, and, as we learned in **Lesson One**, profited financially by it.

Part Two describes the beginnings of a long-running personal rivalry between Crassus and **Pompey**.

Vocabulary

straight: right away

praetor: a Roman magistrate or judge

bewray: reveal

victuals (pronounced "vittles"): food, supplies

great receipt: large size

receiver: in this case, the manager of a property

divers: various people

levy: gather

Imperator: a victorious general

he had no experience in matters of war: this is more to say that Crassus was lacking much experience, than that he had none at all

privily: privately, secretly

before Rome itself: this refers to the place the battle was fought, not the time

privity: agreement

humour of avarice: sense of greed

followed Caesar's hope: pinned their hopes on Caesar

the commonweal or commonwealth: the Roman Republic

manner: custom

People

Sulla: sometimes spelled Sylla. Lucius Cornelius Sulla Felix was a Roman general, and the subject of Plutarch's *Life of Sulla*.

Metellus Pius: Quintus Caecilius Metellus Pius was a Roman general and a supporter of Sulla.

Pompey: Gnaeus Pompeius Magnus or Pompey the Great, a Roman statesman and general, who lived from 106 B.C. to 48 B.C., the subject of Plutarch's *Life of Pompey*.

Cato: Marcus Porcius Cato Uticensis, known as Cato the Younger, the subject of Plutarch's *Life of Marcus Cato*.

Reading

Part One

Cinna and Marius being now of greater power, and coming on directly towards Rome, every man suspected **straight** their coming was for no good to the commonwealth, but as appeared plainly, for the death and destruction of the noblest men of Rome. For it so fell out indeed, that they slew all the chief men they found in the city, among whom Crassus' father and his brother were of the number, and himself being at that time but young, escaped the present danger only by flight. Furthermore, Crassus hearing that they laid wait to take him, and that the tyrants sought him in every place, took three of his friends in his company, and ten servants only, and fled into Spain with all possible speed, where he had been with his father before, and had got some friends when he was **praetor**, and ruled that country. Nevertheless, seeing everybody afraid, and mistrusting Marius' cruelty as if he had been at their doors, he durst not **bewray** himself to any man, but went into the fields, and hid him in a great cave being within the land of one Vibius Piciacus by the sea side, from whence he sent a man of his to this Piciacus, to feel what goodwill he bare him, but specially for that his **victuals** began to fail him. Vibius hearing that Crassus was safe, and had escaped, became very glad of it: and understanding how many persons he had with him, and into what place he was got, went not himself to see him, but called one of his slaves (who was his receiver and occupied that ground for him) and bringing him near the place where Crassus was, commanded him every night to provide meat for supper, to bring it ready dressed to this rock whereunder was the cave, and make no words of it, neither be inquisitive for whom it was, for if he did, he should die for it: and otherwise, for keeping the thing secret as he commanded, he promised to make him a free man. This cave is not far from the sea side, and is closed in round about with two rocks that meet together, which receive a soft cool wind into them. When ye are entered into the cave, it is of a great height within, and in the hollows thereof are many other caves of **great receipt** one within another, and besides that, it neither lacketh light nor water: for there is a well of passing good water running hard by the rock, and the natural rifts of the rocks also receiving the light without, where they meet together, do send it inward into the cave. So that in the day time it is marvellous light, and hath no damp air, but very pure and dry, by reason of the thickness of the rock, which sendeth all the moistness and vapour into that springing well.

Crassus keeping close in this cave, Vibius' **receiver** brought victuals thither daily to relieve him, and his company, but saw not them he brought it to, nor could understand what they were: and yet they saw him plainly, observing the hour and time of his coming when he brought the same. He provided them no more then would even necessarily serve their turn, and yet plenty sufficient to make good cheer withal.

In fine, Crassus (after he had lain hidden in this cave eight months) understanding that Cinna was dead, came out: and so soon as he made himself to be known, there repaired a great number of soldiers unto him, of whom he only chose two thousand five hundred, and with them passed by many cities, and sacked one called Malaca, as **divers** do write, but he flatly denied it, and stoutly contraried them that affirmed it. And afterwards having gotten ships together, [he] went into Africa, to **Metellus Pius**, a man of great fame, and that had already gotten a great army together. Howbeit he tarried not long with Metellus, but jarring with him, went unto Sulla, who welcomed and honored him as much, as any that he had about him.

Sulla afterwards arriving in Italy, intending to employ all the young nobility he had in his company, gave every one of them charge under him, and sent Crassus into the country of the Marsians, to levy men of war there. Crassus desiring certain bands of Sulla to aid him, being driven to pass by his enemies: Sulla answered him angrily again: "I give thee thy father, thy brother, thy friends and kinsmen to aid thee, whom they most wickedly have slain and murdered, and whose deaths I pursue with hot revenge of mine army, upon those bloody murderers that have slain them."

Crassus being nettled with these words, departed thence presently, and stoutly passing through his enemies, **levied** a good number of soldiers: and was ever after ready at Sulla's commandment in all his wars.

Part Two

Here began first (as they say) the strife and contention betwixt him and **Pompey**.

For Pompey being younger than Crassus, and born of a wicked father in Rome, whom the people more hated than ever they did man: came yet to great honour by his valiancy, and by the notable acts he did in the wars at that time. So that Sulla did Pompey that honour many times, which he seldom did unto them that were his elders, nor yet unto those that were his equals: as to rise up when he came towards him, to put off his cap, to call him **Imperator**, as much as "lieutenant general." And this galled Crassus to the heart, although he had no wrong in that Pompey was taken before him, because **he (Crassus) had no experience in matters of war** at that time, and also because these two vices that were bred in him, misery and covetousness, drowned all his virtue and well doing. For at the sack of the city of Tuder, which he took, he **privily** got the most part of the spoil to himself, whereof he was accused before Sulla.

Yet in the last battle of all this civil war (which was the greatest and most dangerous of all other), even **before Rome itself**, the wing that Sulla led was repulsed and overthrown; but Crassus, that led the right wing, overcame his enemies, followed them in chase till midnight, sent Sulla word of his victory, and demanded victuals for his men. But then again he ran into as great defame, for buying or begging the confiscate[d] goods of the outlaws appointed to be slain, for little or nothing. And it is said also, that he made one an outlaw in the country of the Brutians, without Sulla's **privity** or commandment, only to have his goods. But Sulla being told of it, would never after use him in any open service. Surely this is a strange thing, that Crassus [him]self being a great flatterer of other[s], and could creep into any man's favour: was yet himself easy to be won through flattery, of any man that would seek him that way. Furthermore, it is said of him that he had this property: that though himself was as extremely covetous as might be, yet he bitterly reproved and utterly misliked them that had his own **humour of avarice**.

Part Three

Pompey's honour that he attained unto daily, by bearing great charge and rule in the wars, did greatly trouble Crassus: both because he obtained the honour of triumph before he came to be Senator, and also that the Romans commonly called him Pompeius Magnus, to say, "Pompey the Great." Crassus being in place on a time when one said that saw Pompey coming, "See, Pompey the Great is come." "And how great, I pray ye?" said he scornfully.

Howbeit despairing that he could not attain to match him in the wars, he gave himself unto the affairs of the city: and by his pains and industry of pleading, and defending men's causes, by lending of money to them that needed, and by helping of them that sued for any office, or demanded anything else of the people, he attained in the end to the like estimation and authority that Pompey was come unto, by his many noble victories.

And there was one notable thing in either of them. For Pompey's fame and power was greater in Rome, when himself was absent: and contrarywise when he was there present, Crassus oftentimes was better esteemed than he. Pompey carried a great majesty and gravity in his manner of life, would not be seen often of the people, but kept from repairing to open places, and would speak but in few men's causes, and that unwillingly: all to keep his favour and credit whole for himself, when he stood in need to employ the same. Where Crassus' diligence was profitable to many, because he kept continually in the marketplace, and was easy to be repaired unto by any man that required his help, daily following those exercises, endeavouring himself to pleasure every man: so that by this easy access and familiarity, for favour and good will, he grew to exceed the gravity and majesty of Pompey.

But as for the worthiness of their persons, their eloquence of speech, and their good grace and countenance: in all those (it is said) Pompey and Crassus were both alike. And this envy and emulation never carried Crassus away, with any open malice and ill will. For though he was sorry to see Pompey and Caesar honoured above him, yet the worm of ambition never bred malice in him. No, though Caesar when he was taken by pirates in Asia (as he was once) and being kept prisoner cried out aloud: "O Crassus, what joy will this be to thee, when thou shalt hear I am in prison." This notwithstanding, they were afterwards good friends, as it appeareth. For Caesar being ready on a time to depart out of Rome [to be] **praetor** into Spain, and not being able to satisfy his creditors that came flocking all at once about him, to stay and arrest his carriage: Crassus in that time of need forsook him not, but became his surety for the sum of eight hundred and thirty talents.

In fine, all Rome [was] divided into three factions, to wit, of Pompey, Caesar, and Crassus (for as for **Cato**, the estimation they had of his fidelity was greater than his authority: and his virtue more wondered at than practised). Insomuch as the gravest and wisest men took part with Pompey; the liveliest youths, and likeliest to run into desperate attempts, **followed Caesar's hope**. Crassus keeping the midst of the stream, was indifferent to them both, and oftentimes changed his mind and purpose. For in matters of government in the **commonweal**, he neither shewed himself a constant friend, nor a dangerous enemy: but for gain, was easily made friend or foe. So that in a moment they saw him praise and reprove, defend and condemn, the same laws, and the same men.

His estimation grew more, through the people's fear of him: than for any good will they bare him. As appeareth by the answer that one Sicinius (a very busy-headed man, and one that troubled every governor of the **commonweal** in his time) made to one that asked him, why he was not busy with Crassus amongst the rest: and how it happened that he so escaped his hands? "O, said he, he carries hay on his horn." The **manner** was then at Rome, if any man had a cursed bullock that would strike with his horn, to wind hay about his head, that the people might beware of him when they met him.

Narration and Discussion

What irritated Crassus most about the treatment that Pompey received?

Why did Crassus seem unable to win Sulla's full trust and respect? What finally ended his association with Sulla?

Explain this statement: "Surely this is a strange thing, that Crassus [him]self being a great flatterer of other[s], and could creep into any man's favour: was yet himself easy to be won through flattery, of any man that would seek him that way." Dryden translates it this way: "As no man was more cunning than Crassus to ensnare others by flattery, so no man lay more open to it, or swallowed it more greedily than himself." Do you think it is true that those who flatter are most vulnerable to being tricked in the same way?

Lesson Three

Introduction

Have you ever heard of Spartacus, the leader of an attempted slave rebellion? The army he raised did one of the most unheard-of things in history: they took on the Romans in an attempt to fight their way out of Italy (Spartacus was hesitant to try actually taking over Rome). They won several battles, and it seemed they were almost unstoppable, until troops led by Crassus were brought in.

This reading covers the first part of the rebellion; **Lesson Four** will finish the story.

Vocabulary

> **commotion:** Dryden translates this "insurrection," which gives a better picture of something that went beyond just a commotion.
>
> **fencers:** gladiators
>
> **rebate, unrebated foils:** to rebate is to reduce the sharpness of

something; so unrebated would be something at its full sharpness, in this case a foil or fencing sword. **At the sharp** refers to the same thing—no guards or protection.

On a time: One time

three score and eighteen: a score is twenty, so seventy-eight

Bacchus: the god of wine and giver of ecstasy

vile and unseemly: beneath their dignity

mistrusting: suspecting

spials: spies

sergeants that carried the axes: lictors; personal bodyguard

repair: go, return

the consuls: The consuls at this time were Gellius and Lentulus. As well as being political leaders, consuls were the generals of the army.

the Po: the Po river

flying: fleeing, running away

Reading

Part One

The **commotion** of **fencers**, which some call Spartacus' war, their wasting and destroying of Italy, came upon this occasion. In the city of Capua, there was one Lentulus called Sparta-Batiatus, that kept a great number of **fencers** at **unrebated foils**, whom the Romans call *Gladiatores*, whereof the most part were **Gauls** and Thracians. These men were kept locked up, not for any fault they had committed, but only for the wickedness of their master that had bought them, and compelled them by force, one to fight with another **at the sharp**.

On a time, two hundred of them were minded to steal away: but their conspiracy being bewrayed, **three score and eighteen** of them entered into a cook's house, and with the spits and kitchen knives, which there they got, went quite out of the city. By the way they fortuned to meet with carts laden with **fencers'** weapons, that were brought from Capua going to some other city: those they also took by force, and arming themselves therewith, got them then to a strong place of situation. Where amongst themselves they chose three captains, and one Spartacus, a Thracian born (and of those countrymen that go wandering up and down with their herds of beasts, never staying long in a place), they made their general.

This Spartacus was not only valiant, but strong made withal, and endued with more wisdom and honesty, than is commonly found in men of his state and condition: and for civility and good understanding, a man more like to the Grecians, than any of his countrymen commonly be. It is reported that when Spartacus came first to Rome to be sold for a slave, there was found, as he slept, a snake wound about his face. His wife seeing it, being his own countrywoman, and a wise woman besides, possessed with **Bacchus'** spirit of divination: said plainly that it did signify, that one day he should be of great power, much dread, and have very good success. This same woman prophetess was then with him, and followed him likewise when he fled.

Part Two

Now first they overthrew certain soldiers that came out of Capua against them, thinking to take them: and stripping them of their armour and weapons, made them glad to take the **fencers'** weapons, which they threw away as **vile and unseemly**. After that, the Romans sent Clodius [the] praetor against them, with three thousand men. [He] besieged them in their fort, situated upon a hill that had a very steep and narrow ascent unto it, and kept the passage up to them: all the rest of the ground round about it, was nothing but high rocks hanging over, and upon them great store of wild vines. Of them the bondmen cut the strongest strips, and made thereof ladders, like to these ship ladders of ropes, of such a length and so strong, that they reached from the top of the hill even to the very bottom: upon those they all came safely down, saving one that tarried above to throw down their armour after them, who afterwards by the same ladder saved himself last of all. The Romans **mistrusting** no such matter, these bondmen compassed the hill round, assailed them behind, and put them in such a fear with the sudden onset, as they fled upon it every man, and so was their camp taken.

Thereupon divers herdmen and shepherds that kept cattle hard by the hill, joined with the Romans that fled, being strong and hardy men: of which some they armed, and others they used as scouts and **spials** to discover.

[Publius Varinus, the praetor, was now sent against them, whose lieutenant, Furius, with two thousand men, they (the slaves) fought and routed. Then Cossinius was sent with considerable forces, to give his assistance and advice, and him Spartacus missed but very little of capturing in person, as he was bathing at Salinae (the Salt Pits); for he with great difficulty made his escape, while Spartacus possessed himself of his (Cossinius's) baggage, and following the chase with a great slaughter, stormed his camp and took it, where Cossinius himself was slain.]

Spartacus having thus now in sundry battles and encounters overcome the praetor himself, P. Varinus, and at the length taken his **sergeants** from him, **that carried the axes** before him, and his own horse, whereon he (Spartacus) rode himself: was grown then to such a power, as he was dreaded of every man. Yet all this notwithstanding, Spartacus wisely considering his own force, thinking it not good to tarry till he might overcome the power of the Romans: marched with his army towards the Alps, taking it their best way after they had passed them over, every man to **repair** home to his own country, some into Gaul, the rest into Thracia. But his soldiers trusting to their multitude, and persuading themselves to do great things: would not obey him therein, but went again to spoil and overrun all Italy.

The Senate of Rome being in a great perplexity, not only for the shame and dishonour that their men should be overcome in that sort by slaves and rebels, but also for the fear and danger all Italy stood in besides: sent both **the consuls** together, Gellius and Lentulus, as unto as difficult and dangerous a war, as any that could have happened unto them.

This Gellius, one of **the consuls**, setting suddenly upon a band of the Germans, which in bravery and contempt as it were, dispersed themselves from their camp, put them to the sword every man. Lentulus, his colleague and fellow consul on the other side, compassed in Spartacus round with a great army: but Spartacus charged his lieutenants that led the army, gave them battle, overthrew them, and took all their carriage.

Hereupon, marching on still with his army towards the Alps, Cassius the praetor, and governor of Gaul about **the Po**, came against him with an army of ten thousand men. Spartacus joined battle with him, and overcame him. Cassius having lost a great number of his men, with great difficulty saved himself by **flying**.

Narration and Discussion

Why did the slaves begin to rebel against Spartacus when he marched them toward the Alps? Would they have been more successful overall if they had obeyed his orders?

Lesson Four

Introduction

When does a skirmish become an official war, or a bunch of rebels become an army? Would it sound impressive to say that Crassus (or Pompey) won the war against the slaves, or could it somehow be embarrassing?

Vocabulary

fetch a compass about: surround

straitly: strictly

sureties: promises

victual, victuals: food, supplies

pillage: thievery

brackish: salty, briny

morian: North's spelling of **morion**, a kind of open helmet.

compassed them in: surrounded them

divers were suitors for him: Pompey had many supporters

supplies: reinforcements

Reading

Part One

The Senate hearing of Cassius' overthrow, were marvellously offended with the consuls, and sent commandment unto them, to leave off the war: and thereupon gave the whole charge thereof unto Marcus Crassus, who was accompanied in this journey with many noble young gentlemen of honourable houses, both for that he was marvellously esteemed, and also for the good will they bare him.

Now went Crassus from Rome, and camped in Romania, tarrying Spartacus' coming, who was marching thitherward. He sent Mummius, one of his lieutenants, with two legions, to **fetch a compass about** to entrap the enemy behind, **straitly** commanding him to follow Spartacus' rearward, but in no case to offer him skirmish nor battle. But Mummius, notwithstanding this strait commandment, seeing some hope given him to do good, set upon Spartacus, who gave him the overthrow, slew numbers of his men, and more [would have] slain, saving that certain of them saved themselves by flight, having only lost their armour and weapons.

Hereupon Crassus was grievously offended with Mummius, and receiving his soldiers that fled, gave them other armour and weapons: but yet upon **sureties**, that they should keep them better thenceforth, than they had before done.

Now Crassus, of the five hundred that were in the first ranks, and that first fled, them he divided into fifty times ten, and out of every one of those he put one of them to death as the lot fell out: renewing again the ancient discipline of the Romans to punish cowardly soldiers, which of long time before had not been put in use. For it is a kind of death that bringeth open shame withal, and because it is done in the face of the camp, it maketh all the residue afraid to see the terror of this punishment.

Crassus having done execution in this sort upon his men, led his army against Spartacus: who still drew back, until he came to the seaside through the country of the Lucanians, where he found in the straits certain pirates' ships of Cilicia, and there determined to go into Sicilia. And having put two thousand men into Sicily, he then revived the war there of the slaves, which was but in manner newly ended, and lacked small provocation to begin it again.

But these pirates having promised Spartacus to pass him over thither, and also taken gifts of him, deceived him, and brake their promise. Whereupon Spartacus returning back again from the seaside, went and camped within a little isle of the Rhegians. Crassus coming thither to seek him, and perceiving that the nature of the place taught him what he should do: [he] determined with a wall to choke up the bar or channel entering into this little island, both to keep his men occupied from idleness, and his enemies also from **victual**.

This was a marvellous hard and long piece of work; notwithstanding, Crassus finished it beyond all men's expectation in a very short time, and brought a trench from one side of the sea to the other overthwart this bar, which was three hundred furlongs in length, fifteen foot broad, and so many in height: and upon the top of this trench [they] built a high wall, of a marvellous strength, whereof Spartacus at the first made light account, and laughed at it. But when **pillage** began to fail him, and travelling all about the isle for **victuals**, perceiving himself to be shut in with this wall, and that there was no kind of **victuals** to be had within all the compass of the isle: he then took the vantage of a rough boisterous night, the wind being very great, when it snowed exceedingly. [He] set his men a-work, and filled up a piece of the trench (being of a small breadth) with earth, stones, and boughs of trees, whereupon he passed over the third part of his army.

Part Two

Crassus at the first then became afraid, lest Spartacus would have taken his way directly toward Rome: but he was soon put out of that fear, when he heard they were fallen out together, and that a great number of them rebelling against Spartacus, went and camped by themselves by the lake of Lucania, which water by report had this variable property, that at certain times it changeth and becometh very sweet, and at some other times again so salt and **brackish**, as no man can drink it.

Crassus going to set upon them, drove them beyond the lake, but could kill no great number of them, nor follow them very far: because Spartacus came presently to the rescue with his army, who stayed the chase. Crassus had written letters before to the Senate, to call Lucullus home out of Thracia, and Pompey out of Spain, whereof he then repented him, and made all the possible speed he could to end this war, before either of them came thither: knowing, that which of them so ever came to his help, to him would the people give the honor of ending this war, and not to himself. Wherefore he first determined to assail them that had revolted from Spartacus, and camped by themselves: who were led by Caius Canicius, and another called Castus. So Crassus sent six thousand footmen before to take a hill, commanding them to lie as close as they could, that their enemies might not discover them: and so they did, and covered their **morians** and headpieces as well as might be, from being seen. Nevertheless they were discovered by two women doing sacrifice for the safety of their army: and thereupon were all in great hazard of casting away, had not Crassus [immediately appeared], who came in time to their aid, and gave the enemies the cruelest battle that ever they fought in all that war. For there were slain of the slaves at that battle, twelve thousand and three hundred, of which, two only were found hurt in the backs, and all the rest slain in the place of their ranks, valiantly fighting where they were set in battle [ar]ray.

Spartacus, after this overthrow, drew towards the mountains of Petelie, whither Quintus, one of Crassus' lieutenants, and Scrofa his treasurer followed him, still skirmishing with his rearward all the way: yet in fine, Spartacus turned suddenly upon them, made the Romans fly that still harried his men in that sort, and hurt Scrofa, Crassus' treasurer, so sore that he hardly escaped with life. But the vantage they had of the Romans by this overthrow fell out in the end to the utter destruction of Spartacus. For his men thereby, being the most of them fugitive bondmen, grew to such a stoutness and pride of themselves, that they would no more flee from fight, neither yet would they any longer obey their leaders and captains: but by the way as they went, they **compassed them in** with their weapons, and told them, that they should go back again with them whether they would or not, and be brought through Lucania against the Romans.

All this made for Crassus as he wished, for he had received news that Pompey was coming, and that **divers were suitors for him** at

Rome to be sent in this journey, saying, that the last victory of this war was due to him, and that he would dispatch it at a battle, as soon as he came thither. Crassus therefore seeking occasion to fight, lodged as near the enemy as he could, and made his men one day cast a trench, which the bondmen seeking to prevent, came with great fury, and set upon them that wrought. Whereupon fell out a hot skirmish, and still **supplies** came on of either side: so that Spartacus, in the end, perceiving he was forced unto it, put his whole power in battle array.

And when he had set them in order, and that they brought him his horse he was wont to fight on: he drew out his sword, and before them all slew the horse dead in the place, saying: "If it be my fortune to win the field, I know I shall have horse enow to serve my turn: and if I chance to be overcome, then shall I need no more horses."

After that, he flew in among the Romans, thinking to attain to fight with Crassus, but he could not come near him: yet he slew with his own hands two Roman centurions that resisted him. In the end, all his men he had about him, forsook him and fled, so as Spartacus was left alone among his enemies: who, valiantly fighting for his life, was cut in pieces.

Now though Crassus' fortune was very good in this war, and that he had shewed himself a noble and valiant captain, venturing his person in any danger, yet he could not keep Pompey from the honour of ending this war: for the slaves that escaped from this last battle where Spartacus was slain, fell into Pompey's hands, who made an end of all those rebellious rascals. Pompey hereupon wrote to the Senate, that Crassus had overcome the slaves in battle, but that he himself had pulled up that war even by the very roots.

After this Pompey made his entry into Rome, and triumphed for his victory of Sertorius, and the conquest of Spain. Crassus also sued not for the great triumph, neither thought he the small ovation triumph afoot, which they granted him, any honour unto him, for overcoming a few fugitive bondmen.

Narration and Discussion

How was Crassus able to stop Spartacus, when others had failed?

Plutarch says that Crassus was a good general; do you agree? Should he have been honoured for his victory over Spartacus as Pompey was for his victory in Spain? What was the reason the Senate gave for allowing him only an "ovation?"

For older students: The historian Appian includes something in his writing that Plutarch omits: the fact that, at the end of the battle, 6,000 slaves were taken prisoner by Crassus and crucified along the Appian Way from Capua to Rome. Can you give any reason why Plutarch left out this fact? Do you think that including it would give more weight either to the military skill or the cruelty of Crassus?

Lesson Five

Introduction

On-and-off friends...or simply co-conspirators? Pompey and Crassus found they had greater political power when they helped each other, though they continued to be personal rivals. They also discovered someone else who shared their desire for power: Julius Caesar.

Crassus and Pompey were elected consuls in 70 B.C., when Crassus was about 45 years old. In either 60 or 59 B.C. (sources differ on this) they formed the "first triumvirate" with Julius Caesar. Caesar became consul in 59 B.C. and then went off to fight the Gallic Wars.

Vocabulary

furtherance: promotion

[beholden] to him: owing him a debt

dealt friendly: Dryden says "zealously promoted his interest"

at jar: at odds

to find him: to last him

nor took any view or estimate of the people's goods: to assess people's goods for tax purposes was one of the responsibilities of a Censor, so Crassus was not carrying out that duty very well.

was had in some jealousy and mistrust: was mistrusted

conspiracy of Catiline: an election scandal in which Crassus was suspected to have taken part

the let was by mean[s] of his son: he was hindered from exacting revenge by his son

changed garments: mourning clothes

invincible: unconquerable

People

Catulus: Quintus Lutatius Catulus (Capitolinus) (*c.* 120–61 B.C.) , the colleague of Crassus. His father was also a politician named Catulus.

Cicero, Catulus, and Cato: Roman leaders, statesmen. Cicero, a great orator, is the subject of Plutarch's *Life of Cicero.*

Publius Licinius Crassus: one of the two sons of Crassus

Reading

Part One

Now Pompey being called to be consul, Crassus, though he stood in good hope to be chosen consul with him, did yet notwithstanding pray his friendship and **furtherance**. Pompey was very willing to help him, and was ever desirous to make Crassus **[beholden] to him**: whereupon he **dealt friendly** for him, and spake openly in the assembly of the city, that he would no less thank the people to appoint Crassus his companion and fellow consul with him, than for making himself consul. But notwithstanding they were both consuls together in office, their friendship held not, but were ever **at jar**, and the one against the other. So by means of their disagreement, they passed all the time of their consulship without any memorable act done: saving that Crassus made a great sacrifice to Hercules, and kept an open feast for the people of Rome of a thousand tables, and gave to every citizen corn **to find him** three months.

But in the end of their consulship, at a common council [held], there was a knight of Rome called Onatius Aurelius: (a man not greatly known, for that he had no dealings in the state, and kept most in the country) who, getting up to the pulpit for orations, told the people what a vision he had seen in his dream. "Jupiter," said he, "appearing to me this night, willed me to tell you openly, that ye should not put Crassus and Pompey out of their office, before they were reconciled together." He had no sooner spoken the words, but the people commanded them to be friends. Pompey sat still, and said never a word to it. But Crassus rose, and took Pompey by the hand, and turning him to the people, told them aloud: "My Lords of Rome, I do nothing unworthy of myself, to seek Pompey's friendship and favour first, since you yourselves have called him the Great, before he had any hair upon his face, and that ye gave him the honour of triumph, before he was Senator."

And this is all that Crassus did of any account in his consulship. When he was censor also, he passed it over without any act done. For he reformed not the Senate, mustered not the men of war, **nor took any view or estimate of the people's goods**: although **Luctatius Catulus** was his colleague and fellow censor, as gentle a person as any of that time that lived in Rome. Now Crassus at the first entry into his office of censor, going about a cruel and violent act, to bring Egypt to pay tribute to the Romans, Catulus did stoutly withstand him: whereby dissension falling out between them, they both did willingly resign their office. In that great **conspiracy of Catiline**, which in manner overthrew the whole state and commonwealth of Rome, Crassus **was had in some jealousy and mistrust**: because there was one of the confederates that named him for one of them, howbeit they gave no credit unto him. Yet **Cicero** in an oration of his, doth plainly accuse Crassus and Caesar, as confederates with Catiline: howbeit this oration came not forth till they were both dead. And in the oration he made also, when his office and authority of consul ceased, he said: that Crassus came one night to him, and shewed him a letter touching Catiline, certainly confirming the conspiracy then in examination. For which cause Crassus ever after hated him [Cicero]: and that he did not openly revenge it, **the let was by mean[s] of his son.**

For **Publius Crassus** much favouring eloquence, and being given to his book, bare great good will unto Cicero: in such sort, that upon his banishment he put on **changed garments** as Cicero did, and procured many other youths to do the like also, and in fine, persuaded his father to become his [Cicero's] friend.

Part Two

Caesar now returning to Rome from the province he had in government, intended to sue for the consulship: and perceiving that Pompey and Crassus were again **at a jar**, thought thus with himself, that to make the one of them his friend to further his suit, he should but procure the other his enemy. Minding therefore to attain his desire with the favour of them both, [he] sought first the means to make them friends, and persuaded with them, that by their controversy the one seeking the other's undoing, they did thereby but make **Cicero, Catulus, and Cato**, of the greater authority, who of themselves were of no power, if they two joined in friendship together: for making both their friends and factions one, they might rule the state and commonwealth even as they would.

Caesar having by his persuasion reconciled Crassus and Pompey, [they] joining their three powers in one, made themselves **invincible**, which afterwards turned to the destruction of the people and Senate of Rome. For he made them not only greater than they were before, the one by the other's means: but himself also of great power through them. For when they began to favour Caesar, he was straight chosen consul without any denial: and so behaved himself in the consulship, that at the length they gave him charge of great armies, and then sent him to govern the Gauls: which was, as a man may say, [a way] to put him into the castle that should keep all the city in subjection: imagining that they two should make spoil and good booty of the rest, since they had procured him such a government.

Now for Pompey, the cause that made him commit this error was nothing else but his extreme ambition. But as for Crassus, besides his old vice of covetousness rooted in him, he added to that a new avarice and desire of triumphs and victories, which Caesar's fame for prowess and noble acts in wars did throughly kindle in him, that he being otherwise his better in all things, might not yet in that be his inferior: which fury took such hold as it never left him, till it brought him unto an infamous end, and the commonwealth to great misery.

Thus Caesar being come out of his province of Gaul unto Luca, divers Romans went thither to see him, and among other, Pompey and Crassus. They having talked with him in secret, agreed among them to devise to have the whole power of Rome in their hands: so that Caesar should keep his army together, and Crassus and Pompey should take other provinces and armies to them. Now to attain to this, they had no way but one: that Pompey and Crassus should again sue the second time to be consuls, and that Caesar's friends at Rome should stand with them for it, sending also a sufficient number of his soldiers to be there at the day of choosing the consuls.

Narration and Discussion

Why was Pompey so willing to promote the political career of Crassus?

Crassus obviously didn't consider this less-than-memorable decade a complete disaster! In fact, Plutarch says that he was now chasing "a new avarice and desire of triumphs and victories," or as Dryden translates it, "a new passion after trophies and triumphs." What desire was now driving him?

Lesson Six

Introduction

Crassus and Pompey went through two more changes of occupation: a year's consulship together, and then moving on to govern foreign provinces. But like many people who get one nice new thing, Crassus wanted even more. He planned to be not only the richest man in Rome, but also the greatest general the people had ever seen.

Vocabulary

peradventure: perhaps

under colour and countenance of..: under the cover of... (using the office of consul as a front for their own agenda)

succour: help, safety

the pulpit for orations: the place for making speeches

procured for themselves: won the governorship

his hap: his good fortune

vaunts: boasts

ostentation: glamour, "showing off"

conceits: notions

to withstand his departure; to let Crassus of his departure: to prevent him from leaving

People

Lucius Domitius Ahenobarbus: although he was not elected consul at this time, he did win the position the next year (54 B.C.).

Cato: a Roman statesman and in-law of Domitius (see previous lesson)

Reading

Part One

Thereupon Pompey and Crassus returned to Rome to that end, but not without suspicion of their practise: for there ran a rumour in the city, that their meeting of Caesar in Luca was for no good intent. Whereupon, Marcellinus and **Domitius** asked Pompey in open Senate, if he meant to make suit to be consul. Pompey answered them: **peradventure** he did, **peradventure** he did not. They [asked] him again the same question: he answered, he would sue for the good men, not for the evil. Pompey's answers were thought very proud and haughty.

Howbeit Crassus answered more modestly, that if he saw it necessary for the commonwealth, he would sue to be consul: if not, that he would not stand for it. Upon these words, some were so bold [as] to make suit for the consulship, as **Domitius** among other[s].

But afterwards Pompey and Crassus standing openly for it, all the rest left off their suit for fear of them, Domitius only excepted: whom **Cato** so prayed and entreated, as his kinsman and friend, that he made him to seek it. For he persuaded him, that it was to fight for the defense of their liberty, and how that it was not the consulship Crassus and Pompey looked after, but that they went about to bring in a tyranny; and that they sued not for the office, but to get such provinces and armies into their hands as they desired, **under colour and countenance of** the consulship. **Cato** ringing these words into their ears, and believing it certainly to be true as he said, brought Domitius as it were by force into the marketplace, where many honest men joined with them: because they wondered what the matter meant that these two noble men should sue the second time to be consuls, and why they made suit to be joined together, and not to have any other with them, considering there were so many other worthy men, meet to be companion with either of them both in that office.

Pompey fearing he should be prevented of his purpose, fell to commit great outrage and violence. As amongst other [things], when the day came to choose the consuls, Domitius going early in the morning before day, accompanied with his friends to the place where the election should be: his man that carried the torch before him was slain, by some whom Pompey had laid in wait, and many of his company hurt, and among others, **Cato**. And having thus dispersed them, he beset a house round about whither they fled for **succour**, and enclosed them there, until they were both chosen consuls together.

Shortly after they [Crassus and Pompey] came with force to **the pulpit for orations**, and drove Cato out of the market place, and slew some of them that resisted and would not fly. They also then prolonged Caesar's government of the Gauls for five years more, and **procured for themselves** by decree of the people, the countries of Syria and Spain. Again, when they drew lots together, Syria fell to Crassus, and Spain to Pompey.

Every man was glad of their fortune. For the people on the one side were loath Pompey should go far from Rome: and himself also loving his wife well, was glad he had occasion to be so near her, that he might remain the most of his time at Rome. But Crassus of all other rejoiced most at **his hap**, that he should go into Syria: and it appeared plainly that he thought it was the happiest turn that ever came to him, for he would ever be talking of the journey, were he in never so great or strange company. Furthermore, being among his friends and familiars, he would give out such fond boasts of it, as no young man could have made greater **vaunts**: which was clean contrary to his years and nature, having lived all his lifetime as modestly, and with as small **ostentation** as any man living. But then forgetting himself too much, [he] had such fond **conceits** in his head, as he not only hoped after the conquest of Syria, and of the Parthians, but flattered himself that the world should see all that Lucullus had done against King Tigranes, and Pompey against King Mithridates, were but trifles (as a man would say) to that [which] he intended. For he looked to conquer the Bactrians, the Indians, and the great ocean sea toward the East, though in the decree passed by the people there was no mention made of any wars against the Parthians.

Part Two

Now every man saw Crassus' ambition and greedy desire of honour: insomuch as Caesar [him]self wrote unto Crassus out of Gaul, commending his noble intent and forwardness, and wished him to go through therewith. But Atteius, one of the tribunes, being bent against Crassus **to withstand his departure**: (having divers other confederates with him to further his purpose, who much misliked that any man of a bravery and lustiness should make war with any nation or people that had no way offended the Romans, but were their friends and confederates), Crassus fearing this conspiracy, prayed Pompey to assist and accompany him out of the city, because he was of great authority and much reverenced of the people, as it appeared then. For, though multitudes of people were gathered together of purpose **to let Crassus of his departure**, and to cry out upon him: yet when they saw Pompey go before him, with a pleasant smiling countenance, they quieted themselves, and made a lane for them, suffering them to pass on, and said nothing. This notwithstanding, Atteius the tribune stepped before them, and commanded Crassus he should not depart the city, with great protestations if he did the contrary. But perceiving Crassus still held on his way notwithstanding, he commanded then one of the officers to lay hold of him, and to arrest him: howbeit the other tribunes would not suffer the officer to do it. So the sergeant dismissed Crassus.

Then Atteius running towards the gate of the city, got a chafing-dish with coals, and set it in the midst of the street. When Crassus came against it, he cast in certain perfumes, and made sprinklings over it, pronouncing horrible curses, and calling upon terrible and strange names of gods. The Romans say that those manner of curses are very ancient, but yet very secret, and of so great force: as he that is once cursed with that curse can never escape it, nor he that useth it doth ever prosper after it. And therefore few men do use it, and never but upon urgent occasion. But then they much reproved Atteius, for using of these dreadful ceremonies and extreme curses, which were much hurtful to the commonwealth, although he for his country's sake had thus cursed Crassus.

Narration and Discussion

Compare the responses of Pompey and Crassus when they were asked if they would be running for the consulship. What do you think Pompey's answer meant? Why did their responses encourage others to say they would run?

Cato accused them that "they sued not for the office, but to get such provinces and armies into their hands as they desired." What did he mean? Compare this to Jesus' teaching that to be first in God's kingdom, one must be the servant of all. What should motivate a Christian to seek a position of leadership and authority?

Outline Crassus' great plans for conquering the East. What do you think caused him to suddenly become so boastful and conceited about his abilities? Should he have taken more notice of the curses that Atteius called down on him?

Lesson Seven

Introduction

Film stars have become governors and presidents, country singers have started chicken restaurants (or the other way around), and kings have been artists and musicians. Some people are good at more than one thing, and others are not. Although Crassus showed his cleverness as in business, and managed to hold onto political power, he began to show his weaker side as a general.

Vocabulary

threescore and upward: over sixty years old

Euphrates: a major river in the Middle East

Mesopotamia: the area between the Tigris and Euphrates rivers, now part of Iraq

by the drum: Dryden and other translators omit this phrase; it may imply something like "by the pound," or cheaply.

tract (verb): to extend, prolong

in garrison: in lodgings there, as the occupying force

Seleucia: an ancient city on the Tigris river

being borne in hand before: having previously believed

cornet: a calvary officer

People

Publius Crassus: the son of Crassus (see previous lesson)

Arsaces, king of the Parthians: the king at this time was Orodes II, referred to later in the text as **Hyrodes**. This seems to have been an error by Plutarch.

Cassius: Gaius Cassius Longinus, better known as the "lean and hungry" co-conspirator in the assassination of Julius Caesar

Artabazes (also called Artavasdes): king of Armenia, who urged Crassus to invade Parthia by the way of Armenia

Reading

Crassus setting forward notwithstanding, sailed on, and arrived at Brundusium, when winter storms had not left the seas, and he had lost many of his ships: howbeit he landed his army, and marched through the country of Galatia. There he found King Deiotarus, a very old man and yet building a new city. [Crassus], to taunt him prettily, said unto him: "What, O King, begin you to build now in the afternoon?" To whom the king of the Galatians again smiling made answer: "And truly, Sir Captain, you go not very early (methinks) to make war with the Parthians." For indeed Crassus was **threescore and upward**, and yet his face made him seem elder than he was.

But to our story again. Crassus being come into the country, had as good luck as he looked for: for he easily built a bridge upon the river of **Euphrates**, and passed his army over it without any let or trouble. So entering into **Mesopotamia**, [he] received many cities, that of good will yielded themselves unto him.

Howbeit there was one city called Zenodotia, whereof Appolonius was tyrant, where Crassus lost a hundred of his men: thereupon he brought his whole army thither, took it by force, sacked their goods, and sold the prisoners **by the drum**. The Greeks called this city Zenodotia, and for winning of the same Crassus suffered his men to call him Imperator, to say, sovereign captain: which turned to his shame and reproach, and made him to be thought of a base mind, as one that had small hope to attain to great things, making such reckoning of so small a trifle. Thus when he had bestowed seven thousand of his footmen **in garrison**, in those cities that had yielded unto him, and about a thousand horsemen: he returned back to winter in Syria.

Thither came his son **Publius Crassus** to him out of Gaul from Julius Caesar, who had given him [Publius] such honours, as generals of Rome did use to give to valiant soldiers for reward of their good service: and brought unto his father a thousand men of arms, all choice men.

This, methinks, was the greatest fault Crassus committed in all his enterprise of that war. For when he should presently have gone on still, and entered into Babylon and **Seleucia** (cities that were ever enemies unto the Parthians), he **tracted** time, and gave them leisure to prepare to encounter his force when he should come against them. Again they found great fault with him for spending of his time when he lay in Syria, seeming rather to lead a merchant's life, than a chieftain's. For he never saw his army, nor trained them out to any martial exercise, but fell to counting the revenue of the cities, and was many days busily occupied weighing of the gold and silver in the temple of the goddess Hierapolis. And worse than that: he sent to the people, princes, and cities about him, to furnish him with a certain number of men of war, and then he would discharge them for a sum of money. All these things made him to be both ill spoken of, and despised of everybody.

The first token of his ill luck that happened to him, came from this goddess Hierapolis, whom some suppose to be Venus, other say Juno, and others, that she is the mother and chief cause that giveth beginning of moisture to every thing that cometh forth and hath a being, and taught men the original cause also of every good thing. For as Crassus the father, and son both, were coming out of the temple: Crassus the younger fell first on his face, and the father afterwards upon his son.

Likewise as he was gathering his garrisons together, calling them out of the cities into the field, there came ambassadors unto him from **Arsaces, king of the Parthians [see note]**: who delivered him their message in few words, and told him, that if this army he brought came from the Romans to make war with their master, then that he would have no peace nor friendship with them, but would make mortal wars against them. Further, if it were (as he had heard to say) that Crassus against the people's minds of Rome, for his own covetous desire, and peculiar profit, was come in a jollity to make war with the Parthians, and to invade their country: then in that respect Arsaces would deal more favourably, in consideration of Crassus' years, and was contented also to suffer his men to depart with life and goods, whom he took rather to be in prison, than **in garrison** within his cities. Thereto Crassus courageously answered, that he would make them answer in the city of **Seleucia**.

Therewith Vagises, one of the eldest ambassadors, fell a-laughing, and shewing Crassus the palm of his hand, told him thus: "Hair will sooner grow in the palm of my hand, Crassus, than you will come to Seleucia."

In this sort the ambassadors took their leave of Crassus, and returned to their **king Hyrodes**, telling him he was to prepare for war. In the mean space, certain of Crassus' soldiers whom he had left **in garrison** in the cities of Mesopotamia, having escaped marvellous dangerously and with great difficulty, brought him news of importance, having themselves seen the wonderful great camp of the enemy and their manner of fight in the assaults they made to the cities where they lay in garrison. And, as it falleth out commonly among men escaped from any danger making things more fearful and dangerous than they be indeed, they reported that it was [im]possible by flying to save themselves, if they [the Parthians] did follow in chase: neither to overtake them also, if they fled. And further, that they had such kind of arrows as would fly swifter, than a man's eye could discern them, and would pierce through any thing they hit, before a man could tell who shot them. Besides, for the horsemen's weapons they used, that they were such as no armour could possibly hold out: and their armours on the other side made of such a temper and metal, as no force of anything could pierce them through.

The Romans, hearing these news, fell from their former stoutness and courage, **being borne in hand before**, that the Parthians differed nothing at all from the Armenians and Cappadocians, whom Lucullus had overcome and spoiled so oft, that he was weary withal: and they had already made account, that their greatest pains in this war, was but the tediousness of the journey they had to make, and the trouble they should have to follow those men that would not abide them. But then, contrary to expectation, they looked to come to strokes, and to be lustily fought withal.

Hereupon, divers captains and head officers that had charge in the army (among whom **Cassius** the treasurer was one) advised Crassus to stay, and to deliberate in council to know whether he were best to go on, or to remain where he was. The soothsayers themselves did partly let Crassus understand, that the gods shewed no good tokens in all their sacrifices, and were hardly to be pacified. But Crassus gave no ear to them, neither would hear any other that told him as much, but only listened to them that counselled him to make haste.

Yet Crassus' chiefest comfort and encouragement, was of **Artabazes**, king of Armenia, who came to his camp with six thousand horse, which were but only the king's **cornet** and guard. Again he promised him other ten thousand horsemen all armed and barbed, and thirty thousand footmen which he kept continually in pay, and counselled Crassus to enter the Parthians' country upon Armenia's side: because his camp should not only have plenty of victuals, which he would send him out of his country, but for that he should also march in more safety, having a country full of mountains and woods before him, very ill for horsemen, which was the only strength and force of the Parthians. Crassus coldly thanked Artabazes for his goodwill, and all his noble offer of aid: yet told him he would take his journey through Mesopotamia, where he had left many good soldiers of the Romans. And thus departed the king of Armenia from him.

Narration and Discussion

What does Plutarch say that Crassus should have concentrated on during the winter in Syria? What did he do instead?

Why was Crassus so interested in weighing out the treasure in the temple of Hierapolis?

"But Crassus gave no ear to them, neither would hear any other that told him as much, but only listened to them that counselled him to make haste." Dryden says, "But he paid no heed to them, or to anybody who gave any other advice than to proceed." See Proverbs 16:18; 17:10, 12, 24. How do these verses apply to Crassus?

Lesson Eight

Introduction

Through hurricanes and drought, and helped along by a "desert fox" named Ariamnes, the Roman army seemed to be heading for nothing but trouble. Crassus knew his army would be safer moving along the river, but Ariamnes persuaded him to take a detour through the desert. No wonder the eagle on the Roman standard is said to have turned his head backward!

Vocabulary

horse: cavalry

shot and slings: archers and slingers

had been laboured: had been worked on

tracting time: stalling, delaying things

163

when he did but remove into the country...: even when he travelled privately with his own family and goods

sumpter: usually means pack animal, but in this case (because the sumpters are on the camels) I think it refers to the packs themselves

his office: his official duty

hearken: give attention

he dislodged betimes: he rode away early

privity: knowledge

whom he bare in hand: whom he told

broil and tumult: disturbance

People

Cassius: see previous lesson

Surena: Hyrodes' "second man in the kingdom," leading the defense against the Romans

Ariamnes: "an Arab chief," "a cunning and wily fellow," who had once been a friend to the Romans but who now aided the Parthians

Reading

But now as Crassus was passing his army upon the bridge he had made over the river of Euphrates, there fell out sudden strange and terrible cracks of thunder, with fearful flashes of lightning full in the soldiers' faces: moreover, out of a great black cloud came a wonderful storm and tempest of wind upon the bridge, that the marvellous force thereof overthrew a great part of the bridge, and carried it quite away. Besides all this, the place where he appointed to lodge, was twice stricken with two great thunder claps. One of his great horse[s] in like case, being bravely furnished and set out, took the bit in his teeth, and leapt into the river with his rider on his back, who were both drowned, and never seen after.

They say also, that the first eagle and ensign that was to be taken up when they marched, turned back of itself, without any hands laid upon it. Further it fortuned that as they were distributing the victuals unto the soldiers, after they had all passed over the bridge, the first thing that was given them, was salt and water lentils, which the Romans take for a token of death and mourning, because they use it at the funerals of the dead.

After all this, when Crassus was exhorting his soldiers, a word escaped his mouth that troubled the army marvellously. For he told them that he had broken the bridge which he had made over the river of Euphrates, of purpose, because there should not a man of them return back again. Where indeed when he had seen that they took this word in ill part, he should have called it in again, or have declared his meaning, seeing his men so amazed thereat: but he made light of it, he was so willful.

He began to march forward into the country by the river's side, with seven legions of footmen, and [a few less than] four thousand **horse**, and in manner as many **shot and slings** lightly armed. There returned to him certain of his scouts that had viewed the country, and told him there was not an enemy to be seen in the field: howbeit that they had found the track of a marvellous number of horse, which seemed as they were returned back.

Then Crassus first of all began to hope well: and his soldiers also, they fell to despise the Parthians, thinking certainly that they would not come to battle with them. Yet **Cassius** his treasurer ever persuaded him the contrary, and thought it better for him to refresh his army a little in one of the cities where he had his garrison, until such time as he heard more certain news of the enemies: or else that he would march directly towards Seleucia by the river's side, which lay fit for him to victual himself easily by boats that would always follow his camp, and should be sure besides that the enemies could not environ him behind, so that having no way to set upon them but before, they should have none advantage of them.

Crassus going about then to consult of the matter, there came one **Ariamnes** unto him, a captain of the Arabians, a fine subtle fellow, which was the greatest mischief and evil, that fortune could send to Crassus at that present time, to bring him to utter ruin and destruction. For there were some of Crassus' soldiers that had served Pompey before in that country, who knew him very well, and remembered that Pompey had done him great pleasures: whereupon they thought that he bare great good will to the Romans. But Ariamnes **had been laboured** at that time by the king of Parthia's captains, and was won by them to deceive Crassus, and to entice him all he could, to draw him from the river and the woody country, and to bring him into the plain field, where they might compass him in with their horsemen: for they meant nothing less than to fight with the Romans at the sword's point.

This barbarous captain **Ariamnes** coming to Crassus, did highly praise and commend Pompey, as his good lord and benefactor (for he was an excellent-spoken man); and extolled Crassus' army, reproving him that he came so slowly forward, **tracting time** in that sort as he did, preparing himself as though he had need of armour and weapon, and not of feet and hands swift and ready against the enemies: who (for the chiefest of them) had of long time occupied themselves to fly with their best moveables, towards the deserts of Scythia and Hyrcania. "Therefore if you determine," (said he) "to fight, it were good you made haste to meet them, before the king [will] have gathered all his power together. For now you have but **Surena** and Sillaces, two of his lieutenants against you, whom he hath sent before to stay you that you follow him not: and for the king himself, be bold, he meaneth not to trouble you."

But he lied in all. For King Hyrodes had divided his army in two parts at the first, whereof himself took the one, and went to spoil the realm of Armenia, to be revenged of King Artabazes: and with the other he sent Surena against the Romans, not for any contempt he had of Crassus (for it was not likely he would disdain to come to battle with him, being one of the chiefest noble men of Rome, and to think it more honourable to make war with King Artabazes in Armenia); but I think rather he did it of purpose to avoid the greater danger, and to keep far off, that he might with safety see what would happen, and therefore sent Surena before to hazard battle, and to turn the Romans back again.

For Surena was no mean man, but the second person of Parthia next unto the king: in riches, reputation, valour, and experience in wars; the chiefest of his time among all the Parthians, and for execution, no man like him. Surena, **when he did but remove into the country only with his household**, had a thousand camels to carry his **sumpters**, a thousand men of arms armed at all pieces, and as many more besides lightly armed: so that his whole train and court made above ten thousand horse. Further, by the tenure of that land he had by succession from his ancestors, **his office** was at the first proclaiming of any king, to put the royal crown or diadem upon the king's head. Moreover, he had restored King Hyrodes that then reigned, to his crown, who had been before driven out of his realm: and had won him also the great city of Seleucia, himself being the first man that scaled the walls, and overthrew them with his own hands that resisted him. And though he was under thirty years of age, yet they counted him a wise man, as well for his counsel, as his experience, which were the means whereby he overcame Crassus. Who through his rashness and folly at the first, and afterwards for very fear and timorousness, which his misfortune had brought him unto, was easy to be taken and entrapped, by any policy or deceit.

Now this barbarous captain Ariamnes having then brought Crassus to believe all that he said, and drawn him by persuasion from the river of Euphrates, unto a goodly plain country, meeting at the first with very good way, but after with very ill, because they entered into sands where their feet sank deep, and into desert fields where was neither tree nor water, nor any end of them that they could discern by eye, so that not only extreme thirst, and miserable way, marvellously amazed the Romans, but the discomfort of the eye also, when they could see nothing to stay their sight upon: that, above all the rest, wrought their extreme trouble. For, neither far nor near any sight of tree, river, brook, mountain, grass, or green herb appeared within their view, but in truth an endless sea of desert sands on every side, round about their camp. Then began they to suspect that they were betrayed.

Again, when news came that Artabazes, king of Armenia, was kept in his country with a great war King Hyrodes made upon him, which kept him that he could not according to his promise come to aid him, yet that he wished him to draw towards Armenia, that both their armies being joined together they might the better fight with King Hyrodes, [and], if not, that he would always keep the woody country, marching in those valleys and places where his horsemen might be safe, and about the mountains: Crassus was so willful as he would write no answer to it, but angrily told the messenger, that he had no leisure then to **hearken** to the Armenians, but that afterwards he would be revenged well enough of Artabazes' treason.

Cassius, his treasurer, was much offended with Crassus for this answer: howbeit perceiving he could do no good with him, and that he took every thing in evil part he said unto him, he would tell him no more. Notwithstanding, taking Ariamnes this captain of the Arabians aside, he rebuked him roundly, and said: "O thou wretch, what cursed devil hath brought thee to us, and how cunningly hast thou bewitched and charmed Crassus: that thou hast made him bring his army into this endless desert, and to trace this way fitter for an Arabian captain of thieves, than for a general and consul of the Romans?" Ariamnes being crafty and subtle, speaking gently unto Cassius, did comfort him, and prayed him to have patience, and going and coming by the bands, seeming to help the soldiers, he told them merrily: "O my fellows, I believe you think to march through the country of Naples, and look to meet with your pleasant springs, goodly groves of wood, your natural baths, and the good inns round about to refresh you, and do not remember that you pass through the deserts of Arabia and Assyria." And thus did this barbarous captain entertain the Romans awhile: but afterwards **he dislodged betimes**, before he was openly known for a traitor, and yet not without Crassus' **privity**, **whom he bare in hand**, that he would go set some **broil and tumult** in the enemy's camp.

Narration and Discussion

The passage begins with a listing of many "bad omens" that happened around Crassus and his troops at this time. Why did Crassus choose to ignore them? Would it have been better to try to pacify those who were more superstitious than he was, or was he right to say that such things were meaningless and that they should go ahead with their plans?

Plutarch gives two reasons why Crassus was defeated by Surena. "Who through his rashness and folly at the first, and afterwards for very fear and timorousness, which his misfortune had brought him unto, was easy to be taken and entrapped, by any policy or deceit." How might remembering this keep us from similar deceits and defeats?

Writing challenge: write or act out the "O thou wretch" scene between Cassius and Ariamnes.

Lesson Nine

Introduction

If you play checkers, what is your favourite strategy for moving your pieces? Does it work better to bunch them all together, or to line them up across the board? At the Battle of Carrhae, Cassius advised Crassus to spread the army out as wide as possible so that they could not be surrounded; but Crassus changed his mind and moved everyone into a square formation. Which do you think would be more effective against the Parthians? You might even want to get out some checkers to help visualize the story.

Vocabulary

ensigns: standards or flags on poles, but the word is also used to refer to groups of soldiers

being for haste in manner besides himself: being in such a hurry that he could hardly manage it

straited: narrowed

they had abidden: they had withstood

hautboy: a musical instrument

cuirass: a piece of armour that covers the front of the body

at adventure: at random

Historic Occasions

53 B.C.: The Battle of Carrhae

Reading

It is reported that Crassus the very same day came out of his tent not in his coat armour, of scarlet (as the manner was of the Roman generals), but in a black coat: howbeit, remembering himself, he straight changed it again. It is said, moreover, that the ensign bearers when they should march away, had much ado to pluck their **ensigns** out of the ground, they stuck so fast. But Crassus scoffing at the matter, hastened them the more to march forward, compelling the footmen to go as fast as the horsemen, till a few of their scouts came in, whom they had sent to discover: who brought news how the enemies had slain their fellows, and what ado they had themselves to escape with life, and that they were a marvellous great army, and well appointed to give them battle.

This news made all the camp afraid, but Crassus [him]self more than the rest, so as he began to set his men in battle [ar]ray, **being for haste in manner besides himself**. At the first following Cassius' mind, he set his ranks wide, casting his soldiers into a square battle [formation], a good way asunder one from another, because he would take in as much of the plain as he could, to keep the enemies from compassing them in, and so divided the horsemen into the wings. Yet afterwards he changed his mind again, and **straited** the battle of his footmen, fashioning it like a brick, more long than broad, making a front, and shewing their faces every way. For there were twelve cohorts or ensigns embattled on either side, and by every cohort a company of horse, because there should be no place left without aid of horsemen, and that all his battle should be alike defended. Then he gave Cassius the leading of one wing, his son Publius Crassus the other, and himself led the battle in the midst.

In this order they marched forward, till they came to a little brook called Balissus, where there was no great store of water, but yet happily lighted on for the soldiers, for the great thirst and extreme heat **they had abidden** all that painful way, where they had met with no water before. There the most part of Crassus' captains thought best to camp all night, that they might in the meantime find means to know their enemies, what number they were, and how they were armed, that they might fight with them in the morning. But Crassus yielding to his son's and his horsemen's persuasion, who entreated him to march on with his army, and to set upon the enemy presently, commanded that such as would eat, should eat standing, keeping their ranks.

Yet on the sudden, before this commandment could run through the whole army, he commanded them again to march, not fair and softly as when they go to give battle, but with speed, till they spied the enemies, who seemed not to the Romans at the first to be so great a number, neither so bravely armed as they thought they had been. For, concerning their great number, Surena had of purpose hid them, with certain troops he sent before: and to hide their bright armours, he had cast cloaks and beasts' skins upon them. But when both the armies approached near to one another, and that the sign to give charge was lifted up in the air: first they filled the field with a dreadful noise to hear. For the Parthians do not encourage their men to fight with the sound of a horn, neither with trumpets nor **hautboys**, but with great kettle drums hollow within, and about them they hang little bells and copper rings, and with them they all make a noise everywhere together, and it is like a dead sound, mingled as it were with the braying or bellowing of a wild beast, and a fearful noise as if it thundered, knowing that hearing is one of the senses that soonest moveth the heart and spirit of any man, and maketh him soonest besides himself.

The Romans being put in fear with this dead sound, the Parthians straight threw the clothes and coverings from them that hid their armour, and then shewed their bright helmets and **cuirasses** of Margian tempered steel, that glared like fire, and their horses barbed with steel and copper. And Surena also, general of the Parthians, who was as goodly a personage, and as valiant, as any other in all his host, though his beauuty somewhat effeminate, in judgement shewed small likelihood of any such courage: for he painted his face, and wore his hair after the fashion of the Medes, contrary to the manner of the Parthians, who let their hair grow after the fashion of the Tartars, without combing or tricking of them, to appear more terrible to their enemies. The Parthians at the first thought to have set upon the Romans with their pikes, to see if they could break their first ranks. But when they drew near and saw the depth of the Romans' battle standing close together, firmly keeping their ranks: then they gave back, making as though they fled, and dispersed themselves. But the Romans marvelled when they found it contrary, and that it was but a device to environ them on every side. Whereupon Crassus commanded his shot and light armed men to assail them, which they did: but they went not far, they were so beaten in with arrows, and driven to retire to their force of the armed men. And this was the first beginning that both feared and troubled the Romans, when they saw the vehemency and great force of the enemies' shot, which brake their armours, and ran through anything they hit, were it never so hard or soft.

The Parthians thus still drawing back, shot all together on every side, not aforehand, but **at adventure**: for the battle of the Romans stood so near together, as if they would, they could not miss the killing of some. These bowmen drew a great strength, and had big strong bows, which sent the arrows from them with a wonderful force. The Romans by means of these bows were in hard state. For if they kept their ranks, they were grievously wounded: again if they left them, and sought to run upon the Parthians to fight at hand with them, they saw they could do them but little hurt, and yet were very likely to take the greater harm themselves. For, as fast as the Romans came upon them, so fast did the Parthians flee from them, and yet in flying continued still their shooting: which no nation but the Scythians could better do than they, being a matter indeed most greatly to their advantage. For by their flight they best do save themselves, and fighting still, they thereby shun the shame of their flying.

Narration and Discussion

Crassus began this passage in what seemed almost a good mood (in spite of the fact that he almost wore his black robe): he laughed, kept everyone marching, and didn't seem to be worried. When the scouts came to tell them that the enemy was right there and ready to fight, though, he was "struck with amazement" (Dryden) or "besides himself" (North), and didn't seem to know quite what to do. Is it because he trusted Ariamnes that he seemed not to be fully prepared for a battle?

Plutarch says that Crassus yielded to "his son's and his horsemen's persuasion, who entreated him to march on with his army, and to set upon the enemy presently." This is probably the first suggestion we have had that this situation was not entirely Crassus' fault. If he had not been swayed by them, what do you think he might have done? Did he have any other real options at this point?

Lesson Ten

Introduction

From this point on, the story continues the disastrous Battle of Carrhae. Arrows...even especially painful Parthian ones...must run out at some point, thought the Romans. But they had not counted on the arrival of reinforcements.

Vocabulary

faint (verb): falter

targets: shields

onset: attack

five hundred shot: five hundred archers

targets: shields

he put them out in breadth: he stretched them out across the field

beguile: trick

a little room: a tight place

cast themselves away: caused their own deaths

cuirasses, jacks: leather or steel breastplates

divers: some, several

took the Romans' part: was friendly to the Romans

Reading

The Romans still defended themselves, and held it out, so long as they had any hope that the Parthians would leave fighting when they had spent their arrows, or would join battle with them.

But after they understood that there were a great number of camels laden with quivers full of arrows, where the first that had bestowed their arrows fetched about to take new quivers: then Crassus seeing no end of their shot, began to **faint**, and sent to Publius his son, willing him in any case to charge upon the enemies, and to give an **onset**, before they were compassed in on every side.

For it was on Publius' side, that one of the wings of the enemy's battle was nearest unto them, and where they rode up and down to compass them behind. Whereupon Crassus' son taking thirteen hundred horsemen with him (of the which, a thousand were of the men of arms whom Julius Caesar sent) and **five hundred shot**, with eight ensigns of footmen having **targets**, most near to the place where himself then was: **he put them out in breadth**, that wheeling about they might give a charge upon them that rode up and down. But they, seeing him coming, turned straight their horse and fled, either because they met in a marsh, or else of purpose to **beguile** this young Crassus, enticing him thereby as far from his father as they could.

Publius Crassus seeing them fly, cried out, "These men will not abide us," and so spurred on for life after them: so did Censorinus and Megabacchus with him (the one a senator of Rome, a very eloquent man, the other a stout courageous valiant man of war), both of them Crassus' well approved friends, and in manner of his own years. Now the horsemen of the Romans being trained out thus to the chase, their footmen also would not abide behind, nor shew themselves to have less hope, joy, and courage, then their horsemen had. For they thought all had been won, and that there was no more to do, but to follow the chase: till they were gone far from the army, and then they found the deceit.

For the horsemen that fled before them, suddenly turned again, and a number of others besides came and set upon them. Whereupon they stayed, thinking that the enemies perceiving they were so few, would come and fight with them hand to hand. Howbeit they set out against them their men at arms with their barbed horse, and made their light horsemen wheel round about them, keeping none order at all: who galloping up and down the plain, whirled up the sand hills from the bottom with their horse feet, which raised such a wonderful dust, that the Romans could scarce see or speak one to another. For they being shut up into **a little room**, and standing close one to another, were sore wounded with the Parthians' arrows, and died of a cruel lingering death, crying out for anguish and pain they felt: and turning and tormenting themselves upon the sand, they brake the arrows sticking in them. Again, striving by force to pluck out the forked arrowheads, that had pierced far into their bodies through their veins and sinews: thereby they opened their wounds wider, and so **cast themselves away**. Many of them died thus miserably martyred: and such as died not, were not able to defend themselves. Then when Publius Crassus prayed and besought them to charge the men at arms with their barbed horse, they shewed him their hands fast nailed to their targets with arrows, and their feet likewise shot through and nailed to the ground: so as they could neither flee, nor yet defend themselves.

Thereupon himself encouraging his horsemen, went and gave a charge, and did valiantly set upon the enemies, but it was with too great disadvantage, both for offence, and also for defence. For himself and his men with weak and light staves, brake upon them that were armed with **cuirasses** of steel, or stiff leather **jacks**. And the Parthians in contrary manner with mighty strong pikes gave charge upon these Gauls, which were either unarmed, or else but lightly armed. Yet those were they in whom Crassus most trusted, having done wonderful feats of war with them.

For they received the Parthians' pikes in their hands, and took them about the middles, and threw them off their horse, where they lay on the ground, and could not stir for the weight of their harness: and there were **divers** of them also that lighting from their horse, lay under their enemies' horse bellies, and thrust their swords into them. Their horse flinging and bounding in the air for very pain threw their masters under feet, and their enemies one upon another, and in the end fell dead among them. Moreover, extreme heat and thirst did marvelously cumber the Gauls, who were used to abide neither of both: and the most part of their horse were slain, charging with all their power upon the men at arms of the Parthians, and so ran themselves in upon the points of their pikes. At the length, they were driven to retire towards their footmen, and Publius Crassus among them, who was very ill by reason of the wounds he had received.

And seeing a sandhill by chance not far from them, they went thither, and setting their horse in the midst of it, compassed it in round with their targets, thinking by this means to cover and defend themselves the better from the barbarous people: howbeit they found it contrary. For the country being plain, they in the foremost ranks did somewhat cover them behind, but they that were behind, standing higher than they that stood foremost (by reason of the nature of the hill that was highest in the midst) could by no means save themselves, but were all hurt alike, as well the one as the other, bewailing their own misery and misfortune, that must needs die without revenge, or declaration of their valiancy.

At that present time there were two Grecians about Publius Crassus, Hieronymus, and Nicomachus, who dwelt in those quarters, in the city of Carres [Carrhae]: they both counselled P. Crassus to steal away with them, and to fly to a city called Ischnes, that was not far from thence, and **took the Romans' part**. But P. answered them, that there was no death so cruel as could make him forsake them, that died for his sake.

When he had so said, wishing them to save themselves, he embraced them, and took his leave of them: and being very sore hurt with the shot of an arrow through one of his hands, commanded one of his gentlemen to thrust him through with a sword, and so turned his side to him for the purpose. It is reported Censorinus did the like. But Megabacchus slew himself with his own hands, and so did the most part of the gentlemen that were of that company. And for those that were left alive, the Parthians got up the sand hill, and fighting with them, thrust them through with their spears and pikes, and took but five hundred prisoners.

After that, they strake off Publius Crassus' head, and thereupon returned straight to set upon his father Crassus, who was then in this state. Crassus the father, after he had willed his son to charge the enemies, and that one brought him word he had broken them, and pursued the chase: and perceiving also that they that remained in their great battle, did not press upon him so near as they did before, because that a great number of them were gone after the other for rescue: he then began to be lively again, and keeping his men close, retired with them the best he could by a hillside, looking ever that his son would not be long before that he returned from the chase. But Publius seeing himself in danger, had sent **divers** messengers to his father, to advertise him of his distress, whom the Parthians intercepted and slew by the way: and the last messengers he sent, escaping very hardly, brought Crassus news, that his son was but cast away, if he did not presently aid him, and that with a great power.

These news were grievous to Crassus in two respects: first for the fear he had, seeing himself in danger to lose all: and secondly for the vehement desire he had to go to his son's help. Thus he saw in reason all would come to nought, and in fine determined to go with all his power, to the rescue of his son. But in the meantime the enemies were returned from his son's overthrow, with a more dreadful noise and cry of victory than ever before: and thereupon their deadly sounding drums filled the air with their wonderful noise.

The Romans then looked straight for a hot alarm. But the Parthians that brought Publius Crassus' head upon the point of a lance, coming near to the Romans, shewed them his head, and asked them in derision, if they knew what house he was of, and who were his parents: for it is not likely (said they) that so noble and valiant a young man, should be the son of so cowardly a father, as Crassus.

The sight of Publius Crassus' head killed the Romans' hearts more than any other danger they had been in at any time in all the battle. For it did not set their hearts afire as it should have done, with anger, and desire of revenge: but far otherwise, made them quake for fear, and struck them stark dead to behold it.

Yet Crassus [him]self shewed greater courage in this misfortune, than he before had done in all the war beside. For riding by every band he cried out aloud: "The grief and sorrow of this loss (my fellows) is no man's but mine, mine only: but the noble success and honor of Rome remaineth still unvincible, so long as you are yet living. Now, if you pity my loss of so noble and valiant a son, my good soldiers, let me entreat you to turn your sorrow into fury: make them dearly buy the joy they have gotten: be revenged of their cruelty, and let not my misfortune fear you. For why? aspiring minds sometime must needs sustain loss. Lucullus overcame not Tigranes, nor Scipio Antiochus, but their blood did pay for it. Our ancestors in old time lost a thousand ships, yea in Italy **divers** armies and chieftains for the conquest of Sicilia: yet for all the loss of them, at the length they were victorious over them, by whom they were before vanquished. For the Empire of Rome came not to that greatness it now is at, by good fortune only, but by patience and constant suffering of trouble and adversity, never yielding or giving place to any danger."

Narration and Discussion

Why does Plutarch say that Crassus "shewed greater courage in this misfortune, than he before had done in all the war beside," or in Dryden's words, "outdid himself in this calamity?"

Read 2 Samuel 18:24-33 (David's reaction to the death of his son). Note any similarities to the story of Crassus and Publius, though David's relationship with Absalom was somewhat different.

Lesson Eleven

Introduction

The Parthians kindly gave the Romans a night off from fighting; but it was not a night of rest. Attempting to escape their camp without notice, the Romans fell into confusion and disorder; but somehow many of them, including Crassus, did make it to the Roman-ruled town of Carrhae. Might there be a last chance now for Crassus to negotiate peace with the Parthians?

Vocabulary

upon the wings: on either side

the Romans' battle: their battle formation

a narrow room: a tight space

dispatched: killed

Arsaces: the name of the royal house of the Parthians

let their flight: prevent them from escaping

the meanest of all other: the worst off of all

saving three hundred horsemen: except for three hundred horsemen

parle: speak

divers: various

Reading

Crassus using these persuasions to encourage his soldiers for resolution, found that all his words wrought none effect: but contrarily, after he had commanded them to give the shout of battle, he plainly saw their hearts were done, for that their shout rose but faint, and not all alike. The Parthians on the other side, their shout was great, and lustily they rang it out.

Now when they came to join, the Parthians archers a-horseback compassing in the Romans **upon the wings**, shot an infinite number of arrows at their sides. But their men at arms giving charge upon the front of **the Romans' battle** with their great lances, compelled them to draw into **a narrow room**, a few excepted, that valiantly, and in desperate manner ran in among them, as men rather desiring so to die, than to be slain with their arrows, where they could do the Parthians almost no hurt at all. So were they soon **dispatched**, with the great lances that ran them through, head, wood and all, with such a force, as oftentimes they ran through two at once.

Thus when they had fought the whole day, night drew on, and made them [the Parthians] retire, saying they would give Crassus that night's respite, to lament and bewail his son's death: unless that otherwise he, wisely looking about him, thought it better for his safety to come and offer himself to **King Arsaces'** mercy, than to tarry [and] to be brought unto him by force. So the Parthians camping hard by the Romans, were in very good hope to overthrow him the next morning.

The Romans on the other side had a marvellous ill night, making no reckoning to bury their dead, nor to dress their wounded men, that died in miserable pain: but every man bewailed his hard fortune, when they saw not one of them could escape, if they tarried till the morning. On the other side, to depart in the night through that desert, their wounded men did grieve them much, because, to carry them so away, they knew it would **let their flight**: and yet to leave them so behind, their pitiful cries would give the enemies knowledge of their departure.

Now, though they all thought Crassus the only author of their misery, yet were they desirous to see his face, and to hear him speak. But Crassus went aside without light, and laid him down with his head covered, because he would see no man, shewing thereby the common sort an example of unstable fortune: and the wise men, a good learning to know the fruits of ill counsel, and vain ambition, that had so much blinded him, as he could not be content to command so many thousands of men, but thought (as a man would say) himself **the meanest of all other**, and one that possessed nothing, because he was accounted inferior unto two persons only, Pompey and Caesar.

Notwithstanding, Octavius, one of his chieftains, and Cassius the treasurer, made him rise, and sought to comfort him the best they could. But in the end, seeing him so overcome with sorrow, and out of heart, that he had no life nor spirit in him: they themselves called the captains and centurions together, and sat in council for their departure, and so agreed that there was no longer tarrying for them. Thus of their own authority at the first they made the army march away, without any sound of trumpet or other noise.

But immediately after, they that were left hurt and sick, and could not follow, seeing the camp remove, fell a-crying out and tormenting themselves in such sort, that they filled the whole camp with sorrow, and put them out of all order, with the great moan and loud lamentation: so as the foremost rank that first dislodged, fell into a marvellous fear, thinking they had been the enemies that had come and set upon them. [By which means, now and then turning out of their way, now and then standing to their ranks, sometimes taking up the wounded that followed, sometimes laying them down, they wasted the time], **saving three hundred horsemen** that escaped, who came about midnight to the city of Carres [Carrhae].

Ignatius, their captain, called to the watch on the walls, and spake in the Latin tongue. Who answering, he willed them to tell Coponius, governor of the town, that Crassus had fought a great battle with the Parthians, and said no more, neither told what he was: but rode on still, till he came to the bridge which Crassus had made over [the] Euphrates. Yet this word Ignatius gave to the watch to tell Coponius, served Crassus' turn very well. For Coponius thought by this great haste of his, and the short confused speech he made, passing on his way, that he had no good news to tell them: wherefore he straight armed his soldiers, and understanding that Crassus was returning back, went to meet him, and brought him and his army into the city of Carres.

The Parthians knew well enough of the removing of the Romans' camp, but yet would not follow them in the night, but the next morning entering into their camp where they lay, slew all that were left behind, which were about four thousand men: and riding after them that were gone, took many stragglers in the plain. Among them there was Barguntinus, one of Crassus' lieutenants, who strayed in the night out of the army with four whole ensigns, and having lost his way, got to a hill, where the Parthians besieged him, slew him and all his company, though he valiantly there defended himself: yet twenty of them only escaped, who with their swords drawn in their hands, running forward with their heads, thrust in among the thickest of the Parthians: they wondering at their desperation, opened [their ranks], and suffered them to march on towards the city of Carres.

In the mean time false news was brought to Surena, how Crassus with all the chiefest men of his host was fled, and that the great number that were received into the city of Carres were men of all sorts gathered together, and not a man of any quality or estimation. Surena thereupon thinking he had lost the honour of his victory, yet standing in some doubt of it, because he would know the truth, that he might either besiege the city of Carres, or pursue after Crassus: sent one of his interpreters to the walls of the city, charging him to call for Crassus, or Cassius, and to tell them that Surena would **parle** with them.

The interpreter did as he was commanded. Word was brought to Crassus, and he accepted **parlance**. Shortly after also, thither came certain soldiers of the Arabians from the camp of the Parthians, who knew Crassus and Cassius very well by sight, having **divers** times seen them in their camp before the battle. These Arabians seeing Cassius upon the walls, told him, that Surena was contented to make peace with them, and to let them go safely, as his master's good friends, so that they would surrender Mesopotamia into the king of Parthia's hands, and how they thought that was the best way for both parties, rather than to be enforced unto it by extremity. Cassius thought this a good offer, and told them, that they must appoint the day and place, where Crassus and Surena should meet to talk together of the matter. The Arabians made answer they would do it: and so departed. Surena, hearing this, was glad he had them at such advantage, where he might besiege them.

Narration and Discussion

"But Crassus went aside without light, and laid him down with his head covered, because he would see no man, shewing thereby the common sort an example of unstable fortune." Dryden says, "But he wrapped his cloak around him, and hid himself, where he lay as an example of inconsiderateness and ambition . . . " Discuss this sentence. What is Plutarch saying about the character of Crassus?

What do you think of Cassius's eagerness to have Crassus meet with Surena? Is he perhaps too trusting?

Lesson Twelve

Introduction

Do you remember Ariamnes, "the most faithless of men?" Another guide, Andromachus, appears in this last passage as the Romans' guide out of Carrhae, and, with the same degree of helpfulness as Ariamnes, he leads them in circles while keeping the Parthians well informed of their every move.

Vocabulary

no boot: no use

advertised: informed

sign of Sagittary (Sagittarius): Sagittarius is symbolized by an archer.

sergeants that carried the axes and rods before him: lictors; his bodyguard

to give colour to this bruit: to sell his story

crafty fetches and devices: tricks

beating of their harness: Dryden says they "clashed their targets" to make a noise of protest.

mongrel: half-breed

capitulations: things agreed to give up; terms of surrender

perjury: lies

deserts: what they deserved

Reading

Part One

The next day [Surena] brought all his army before the city of Carres. There the Parthians marvelously reviled the Romans, and told them, they must deliver them Crassus and Cassius bound hands and feet, if they would have any grace or peace with them.

The Romans were marvelously offended that they were thus deceived, and told Crassus, that it was **no boot** any longer to look for aid of the Armenians, but presently to flee: howbeit to keep it secret in any wise from any of the Carrenians, till the very hour of their departure. Yet Crassus [him]self had told it to Andromachus, the veriest traitor and villain in all the city, whom he had chosen to be his guide. This traitor Andromachus advertised the enemies, in every point, of their purpose and departure. But because the Parthians [did] never use to fight in the night, and that it was a hard matter to bring them to it, and again that Crassus departed in the night time: Andromachus was afraid least the Romans would win such ground before the Parthians, as they could not possibly overtake him the next day. Therefore of purpose he sometimes brought them one way, other while another way, and at the last, brought them into a great bog or marsh, full of deep holes and ditches, and where they must needs make many turns and returns before they could get out again, and yet very hardly.

Whereupon, some in the army began to mistrust, that Andromachus meant no good to turn and toss them up and down in that sort, and therefore would follow him no more: insomuch as Cassius among others, returned towards the city of Carres again, from whence they came. And when his guides (who were Arabians) counselled him to tarry there, till the moon were out of the sign of Scorpio, he answered them: "I fear **the sign of Sagittary** more."

So as soon as he could, he took his way towards Assyria with five hundred horsemen. And other[s] of the army also having faithful guides, recovered a country of the mountains, called Sinnaca, and retired into a safe place before the break of day: and they were about five hundred men, whom Octavius, a noble man, had in charge.

But the day stole upon Crassus, hunting up and down yet in the marsh, in those ill-favoured places, into the which Andromachus that traitor had of purpose brought him, having with him four ensigns of footmen all with targets, and very few horsemen, and five **sergeants that carried the axes and rods before him**: with whom, with much ado and great labour, he got into the right way, when the enemies were almost upon him, and that he was within twelve furlong[s] of joining with Octavius. There in haste he had gotten a hill, which was not so steep for horsemen, neither of such strength as the other hills were, called Sinnaces, yet under them, and joining to them by a long hill that runneth alongst the plain, so as Octavius plainly saw the danger Crassus was in. Thereupon he first ran down the hills with a few of his men that followed him: but after also came all the rest, saying they were cowards if they should tarry behind.

At their coming they gave such a hot onset upon the Parthians, that they made them give back from that hill: and compassing Crassus in the midst of them, covering him round with their targets, they spake nobly, that never [an] arrow of the Parthians should touch the body of their general, before they were slain one after another, and that they had fought it out to the last man in his defence.

Part Two

Hereupon Surena perceiving the Parthians were not so courageous as they were wont to be, and that if night came upon them, and that the Romans did once recover the high mountains, they could never possibly be met withal again: he thought cunningly to beguile Crassus once more by this device. He let certain prisoners go of purpose, before whom he made his men give out this speech: that the king of Parthia would have no mortal war with the Romans; but far otherwise, he rather desired their friendship, by shewing them some notable favour, as to use Crassus very courteously. And **to give colour to this bruit**, he called his men from fight, and going himself in person towards Crassus, with the chiefest of the nobility of his host, in quiet manner, his bow unbent: he held out his right hand, and called Crassus to talk with him of peace, and said unto him [that] though the Romans had felt the force and power of their king, it was against his will, for he could do no less but defend himself: howbeit that now he was very willing and desirous to make them taste of his mercy and clemency, and was contented to make peace with them, and to let them go safely where they would.

All the Romans besides Crassus were glad of Surena's words. But Crassus that had been deceived before by their **crafty fetches and devices**, considering also no cause apparent to make them change thus suddenly: would not hearken to it, but first consulted with his friends. Howbeit the soldiers cried out on him to go, and fell at words with him, saying that he cared not though they were all slain, and that himself had not the heart only to come down and talk with the enemies that were unarmed.

Crassus proved first to pacify them by fair means, persuading them to bear a litle patience but till night, which was at hand, and then they might safely depart at their pleasure, and recover the mountains and strait passages, where their enemies could not follow them: and pointing them the way with his finger, he prayed them not to be faint hearted, nor to despair of their safety, seeing they were so near it. But in the end Crassus perceiving they fell to mutiny, and, **beating of their harness**, did threaten him if he went not, fearing then they would do him some villainy: [he] went towards the enemy, and coming back a little, said only these words: "O Octavius, and you, Petronius, with all you Roman gentlemen that have charge in this army: you all see now how against my will I am enforced to go to the place I would not, and can witness with me, how I am driven with shame and force. Yet I pray you if your fortunes be to escape this danger, that ye will report wheresoever you come, that Crassus was slain, not delivered up by his own soldiers into the hands of the barbarous people, as I am: but deceived by the fraud and subtlety of his enemies."

Part Three

Octavius would not tarry behind on the hill, but went down with Crassus: but Crassus sent away his officers that followed him. The first that came from the Parthians unto Crassus were two **mongrel**

Grecians who, dismounting from their horse, saluted him, and prayed him to send some of his men before, and Surena would shew them, that both himself and his train came unarmed towards him. Crassus thereto made them answer, that if he had made any account of his life, he would not have put himself into their hands.

Notwithstanding he sent two brethren before, called the Roscians, to know what number of men, and to what end they met so many together. These two brethren came no sooner to Surena, but they were stayed: and himself in the meantime kept on his way a-horseback, with the noblest men of his army. Now when Surena came near to Crassus: "Why, how now," (quoth he) "what meaneth this? a consul and lieutenant general of Rome afoot, and we a-horseback?" Therewithal he straight commanded one of his men to bring him a horse. Crassus answered Surena again, [saying that] in that, they neither of both offended, following the use and manner of their country, when any meeting is made for treaty of peace.

Surena replied: "As for the treaty of peace, that was already agreed upon between the King Hyrodes, and the Romans: howbeit that they were to go to the river, and there to set down the articles in writing. For you Romans," said he, "do not greatly remember the **capitulations** you have agreed upon." With those words he gave him his right hand. As Crassus was sending for a horse: "You shall not need," said Surena, "for look, the king doth present you this." And straight [away] one was brought him with a steel saddle richly gilt, upon the which his gentlemen mounted Crassus immediately, and following him behind, lashed his horse to make him run the swifter.

Octavius, seeing that, first laid hand on the bridle; then Petronius, colonel of a thousand footmen; and after them, all the rest of the Romans also gathered about Crassus to stay the horse, and to take him from them by force, that pressed him on of either side. So they thrust one at another at the first very angrily, and at the last fell to blows.

Then Octavius drew out his sword, and slew one of the barbarous noblemen's horsekeepers: and another came behind him, and slew Octavius. Petronius had no target, and receiving a blow on his cuirass, lighted from his horse, and had no hurt: and on the other side came Pomaxathres, one of the Parthians, and slew Crassus. Some say, notwithstanding, that Pomaxathres slew him not, but another, yet that he cut off his head and his hand after he fell dead to the ground. But all these reports are rather conjectures, than any certainty.

For as for them that were there, some of them were slain in the field fighting for Crassus, and other saved themselves by flying to the hill. The Parthians followed them, and told them that Crassus had paid the pain he had deserved: and for the rest, that Surena bade them come down with safety. Then some of them yielded to their enemies: and other dispersed themselves when night came, and of them very few escaped with life. Other being followed and pursued by the Arabians were all put to the sword. So as it is thought there were slain in this overthrow, about twenty thousand men, and ten thousand taken prisoners.

Such was the success of Crassus' enterprise and voyage, much like unto the end of a tragedy. But afterwards, Hyrodes' cruelty, and Surena's foul **perjury** and craft, were in the end justly revenged upon them both, according to their **deserts**. For King Hyrodes, envying Surena's glory, put Surena to death. And Hyrodes [was murdered by his son].

Narration and Discussion

Discuss Crassus' statement: "Yet I pray you if your fortunes be to escape this danger, that ye will report wheresoever you come, that Crassus was slain, not delivered up by his own soldiers into the hands of the barbarous people, as I am: but deceived by the fraud and subtlety of his enemies." Dryden translates this, "Tell all men when you have escaped, that Crassus perished rather by the subtlety of his enemies, than by the disobedience of his countrymen." Is this true? Why did he want this said about him?

Final lesson summary: What ideas about Crassus do you think Plutarch tried to get across in the story of his life? Is there something we can copy, or something to be avoided? Is he to be admired, faulted, or pitied?

Bibliography

Plutarch's Lives of the Noble Greeks and Romans. Englished by Sir Thomas North. With an introduction by George Wyndham. Third Volume. London: Dent, 1894. (Pyrrus)
https://archive.org/details/livesenglishedb03plut

Plutarch's Lives of the Noble Greeks and Romans. Englished by Sir Thomas North. With an introduction by George Wyndham. Fourth Volume. London: Dent, 1894. (Nicias, Marcus Crassus)
https://archive.org/details/livesenglishedb04plut

Plutarch's Lives: The Dryden Plutarch. Revised by Arthur Hugh Clough. Volume 2. London: J.M. Dent, 1910. (Pyrrhus)
https://archive.org/details/plutarchslives02plut

Plutarch's Lives: The Dryden Plutarch. Revised by Arthur Hugh Clough. Volume 3. London: J.M. Dent, 1910. (Nicias, Crassus)
https://archive.org/details/plutarchslives03plut

About the Author

Anne E. White (www.annewrites.ca) has shared her knowledge of Charlotte Mason's methods through magazine columns, online writing, and conference workshops. She is an Advisory member of AmblesideOnline, and the author of *Minds More Awake: The Vision of Charlotte Mason*, as well as other books in The Plutarch Project series.